karma101

FAIR WINDS
PRESS
GLOUCESTER, MASSACHUSETTS

karma101

what goes around comes around . . .

and what you can do about it

JOSHUA MACK

First published in the U.S.A. in 2002 by
Fair Winds Press
33 Commercial Street
Gloucester, Massachusetts 01930-5089

Library of Congress Cataloging-in-Publication Data
Mack, Joshua.
    Karma 101 : what goes around comes around—
and what you can do about it / Joshua Mack.
        p.   cm.
    ISBN 1-931412-19-7
    1. Causation (Buddhism) 2. Karma. I. Title.
BQ4240 .M32 2002
291.2'2—dc21   2002007883

10 9 8 7 6 5 4 3 2 1

Design by John Hall Design Group

Printed in Canada

For Linda

ACKNOWLEDGMENTS

THERE ARE COUNTLESS PEOPLE I would like to thank for helping me, in one way or another, with this book. To name them all would be a book in itself. Briefly, I would like to thank my editor, Wendy Simard, who put up with more than I can imagine yet stayed the course, and whose faith made this a reality; Ron Leifer, whose wisdom and kindness served as a guide and an education through difficult times and whose lessons still weave through my brain to this day; Alyssa Bost, whose infinite patience, support, ideas, and perspective not only kept me kept me afloat but convinced me on more than one occasion that launching my laptop into the lake would solve nothing; and my dog, Max, a true companion and free spirit who has weathered it all and been the most stable fixture in my front passenger seat during the ride.

CONTENTS

YOU'RE IN A RUSH, frustrated with the speed of traffic, and weaving in and out of lanes when you get stuck behind a guy traveling with the speed of an oxcart. You begin to seethe, fantasizing about the pleasure of plowing into him. With a quick flash of your lights and a curse to make your mother cringe, you abruptly pull out and cut the guy off on your right, the quick acceleration causing your coffee, precariously balanced on the dash, to spill on your lap before you catch the cup. Now you're wet, frustrated, the guy behind you is shooting daggers through your back, and perhaps worst of all, your precious elixir, with the exception of the soon-to-be cold quarter of an inch left in the mug, is gone. From the passenger seat, your friend acts profound: "Ahh, the joys of karma."

But what is karma? Punishment? Payback through divine intervention? Did the universe just catch you with your hand in the cookie jar? Were you a creep in a past life and this is your lot? Is it fate? Pop culture has largely adopted a kind of fast-food version of karma, making it a great one-liner and a good thing to say with a shrug and your hands in the air. Karma, however, can be like time, the phenomenon St. Augustine said he felt certain he understood perfectly—until someone asked him.

It's Organic

The fact of the matter is that karma is actually *not* a very mysterious concept; there are no logarithms, numbers, or mind-numbing formulas to work out in order to get a good grasp of it. At its most basic, karma is simply a natural law of cause and effect. Perhaps the biggest mental hurdle the Western mind faces in understanding the true workings of karma is to adjust to a view that assumes that all of us and the universe are all part of one, big, organic whole, in which everything is interrelated and in which everything *affects* everything: You do something and you have an effect, something happens and there is a result, you pulled a fiver out of your mother's purse when you were 16 and now your kid will probably do the same to you, a butterfly flaps its wings in Japan and the weather changes in Chicago.

Karma is not a moral law. It is neutral; it is only a description of how things interact. Karma is not a force wielded by the gods, nor is it the result of divine intervention. Karma does not think, karma is not watching you, karma does not keep a list and check it twice. You generate your own karma, you are your own karma, you are the sum result of your previous actions and thoughts. Bottom line: You are in control of your own karma.

What Goes Around...

When you talk behind someone's back and the next time you see them they're looking at you funny, things have come full circle. When you steal a parking spot from another driver and the next time a person does the same to you, things have come full circle. When you lend a quarter to someone on the street who needs to use the pay phone and two weeks later someone lends you bus fare after you discover your pockets are empty, things have come full circle. The results of what you do might not be immediately apparent, but there is nothing you can do that won't affect something. The day in third grade when you and a few friends pinned the geek down and gave him a wedgie may have been the impulse that led him to become a green beret 20 years later. The pity you felt when watching the worms struggle on the sidewalks during a rainstorm as a kid may have helped contribute to your desire to become a doctor so you could save lives and help those who suffer.

We're All Related

Modern science is rapidly coming closer to adopting a perspective of the world and universe as being inextricably interconnected, in which everything affects everything and nothing is separate. Understanding karma is about understanding the effects your actions have on yourself, others, and, ultimately, on everything. Despite emotions that might make us feel differently, none of us are in reality lone actors—our lives are full of daily interactions with others in which we add our own influence to the manner in which the day will unfold. By not participating we are also acting—we are *actively* not acting. We all have an impact. Whether it's smiling at the person about to take your order, which makes them smile, or giving them a scowl, which makes it more likely they'll spit in your soup next time, you are always doing things that shape the course of the day and your life.

Karmic Myths

In the past, karma often received a bad rap in the West as being synonymous with either fate or destiny or some "New Age" thing—a brand name of an herbal remedy line you'd find in an organic health food store your parents would be scared to be seen in. But when we look at something and try to understand it, we do so through the methods and with the attitudes with which we've been conditioned; trying to understand karma solely by reading the small description on the back of the menu at the Karma restaurant can be like trying to appreciate the color green while looking through orange-colored sunglasses. This book is an attempt to lay bare the basics of karma, to strip it down to its bare minimum and make it tangible, bringing it out of antiquity to watch it play out in the context of your local Starbucks, your mother in-law's, the movie theater—your life.

Karma Culture

Cultures and modes of thought don't arise from—or exist—in vacuums. For example, many of the initial seeds of Greek thought, which went on to form the basis for Western philosophy and science, were borrowed from the Egyptians in the sixth century B.C.E. So although there can be no doubt that there have been traces and influences of Eastern thought in the West since time immemorial, and Western writers such as Ralph Waldo Emerson were introducing Eastern concepts such as karma in the mid-nineteenth century, it was not until the mid-twentieth century, during the American Zen Boom, that the staples of Eastern thought and philosophy began having a direct impact on the Western psyche. By the

1960s, karma had become a cultural hit, and by the 80s and 90s all things East had become hip and even profitable; yoga was a fad that went as well with meditation as it did with a Diet Pepsi.

Before anyone gets too rattled, it should be made clear that when discussing anything, be it music, movies, art, or the behavior of your aunt's six-year-old kid, labels and categories are necessary in order to impart meaning. Therefore, in the following pages, the distinction is repeatedly made between Eastern thought and Western thought. Obviously, not everyone in the East thinks "like this," nor does everyone in the West think "like that," but based on the historical paths of philosophy that have been taken in the respective regions, the categories still hold up well enough to be useful (though that would seem to be changing).

Furthermore, it's important to understand that karma is merely a name for a phenomenon, like gravity. It is not the name, per se, that is so important, but understanding the phenomenon itself. As Shakespeare said, "What's in a name? That which we call a rose, by any other name would smell as sweet." To that end, we can avoid falling prey to the typical dogmatic pitfalls by remembering that what we are interested in is more the action and workings of karma than in some blind belief in karma itself.

What Is Karma?

Whatever we do, with our body, speech, or mind, will have a corresponding result. Each action, even the smallest, is pregnant with its consequences.

—Sogyal Rinpoche, author of *The Tibetan Book of Living and Dying*

CASE STUDY

Singin' the Porta-Potty Blues

STEVE WAS AN ARROGANT MAN, an insecure man, the kind of man who likes to appear important and makes a point of casually name-dropping the brand of suit currently adorning his body. He didn't like to get dirty, obsessively filed his nails, and, of course, was completely unable to take himself lightly. Dragged to an outdoor country music festival by his wife, he was doing his best to seem uninterested and conspicuously hummed Bach at the concession stand.

Despite his wife's urgings, he would do no more than occasionally tap his foot, and even when he did like what he heard, he remained still for fear of looking foolish. Several hours into the show and after four iced teas, Steve had the urge and went to use the porta-potty. When it finally became his turn, he entered the one on the end, which sat on a slight grade, wondering how long he'd be able to hold his breath.

Sitting down, the unthinkable—but cosmically necessary—event occurred. The porta-potty tipped over and landed with a bang—door side down. After a few yelps and a couple of failed attempts to rock the less than cooperative container over by himself, several people joined forces and managed to roll it onto its side. Mr. Fastidious emerged from the plastic tank, expensive suit and ego covered in dietary remains.

Moral of the story: Eventually, everyone comes face to face with his or her own karma.

Karma in Historical Context

One generation plants the trees;
another gets the shade.

—Chinese Proverb

TAKE ANY SLICE OF HISTORY and there's going to be something amazing about the time period you look at. Whether it was the invention of the wheel, the written word, trigonometry, disco, microwave popcorn, or resealable tuna in a pouch that keeps for a week, every age has had its unique and, based on what came before, inevitably mind-boggling developments. The origins of karma are no different. Although it's difficult to pinpoint the exact time and place where the concept came into being, by looking back some 2,600 years ago, we can see that Greeks, Hindus, and Buddhists all shared a world-view that formed the concept of karma.

In the Beginning

The sixth century B.C.E. was an age in which there was as yet no distinction between the metaphysical and the phys-ical, between religion and science, or between alive and inanimate. The general interpretation was that the universe and everything in it existed as a singular unity. Human perceptions of the universe as being composed of separate and distinct entities that could be categorized and controlled were believed to be an illusion.

The Greek Connection

The Greek philosopher Heraclitus believed the natural state of the world to be one of change and thus one of impermanence. He called this state of change that governed the universe "Logos," or "Rule," and somewhat similar to the Taoist idea of the yin and the yang, believed Logos ruled the world through the harmony of opposites existing together; therefore good and bad, love and hate, or boy bands and Bob Dylan are simply two sides of the same coin. Opposites interacted to regulate and maintain the inherent rhythm of nature. Since the reality of the universe is change, Heraclitus didn't buy into the idea of something being static and unchanging.

By Way of the Hindu

Hinduism was already well established in India and also suggested a basic unity of all things, known as Brahman. Similar to the Greek view, any categorization of the world based on separateness was dismissed. The deity Shiva, the creator and the destroyer of a timeless universe, was simply one manifestation of Brahmin. Shiva was seen as the director of a play—the "play" of the world, called *lila*, in which we are all characters. If we believe the play to be real, we are not seeing things as they really are. As long as we are bound by our characters, we are bound to generate karma. According to Hindu beliefs, salvation is to be had by transcending the play, seeing through the theatrics, and then experiencing reunion with the ultimate Brahman.

The Baby Buddha

Buddhism, founded by the Buddha in India in the sixth century B.C.E., can be seen as a variation on both the Greek and the Hindu view. If you can call Hinduism mystical and Greek philosophy the precursor to modern science, Buddhism represents a sort of bridge between both. Similar to the Milesian school, it assumes no gods or deities, but like Hinduism, it does assume that human-made categories and distinctions of reality are an illusion of the true essential nature of the universe. Again, salvation, or truth, can be found by transcending the illusion and experiencing the unity that is the true nature of the universe. And as with Hinduism,

KARMIC
DO
....
Giving hugs for the hell of it.

KARMIC
DON'T
....
Giving hugs only after careful deliberation of the potential costs and benefits.

Buddhists believe it is through our karma that we remain chained to the illusion of separateness, and thus chained to our suffering.

Standing at the Crossroads

All three modes of thought—Greek, Hindu, and Buddhist—thus assumed that nothing existed other than the whole. There was no tangible difference between body and spirit, and the goal of humans was to realize and then experience this unity on a constant basis. What is interesting, however, was that although the East and West may at this point have been on a similar philosophical track, a split was about to take place.

Whereas Western science believed in categories and the separation of mind and matter to expose the truth, the East saw these as constructions and thus illusions masking the true real wholeness of the cosmos and all within it. Western science can be seen as constructing a map to represent the universe, believing that the way to knowledge is through objective separation between the observer and the observed. Eastern philosophy espouses

KARMIC DO

Offering to split that last piece of cake with your friend.

KARMIC DON'T

Going for thirds before anyone else has had seconds.

the belief that the map is not the territory: You can look at a map, but you can't know its real truth unless you merge with it and experience it. This is exactly what has been demonstrated in modern physics: There is no way to actually separate yourself from whatever it is that you are observing and not have a direct effect on it; your very presence influences the results.

The Middle Path

Buddhism is often heralded as offering a successful bridge between science and religion. While Hinduism is mystical and faith-oriented, Buddhism is psychological and empirically oriented. Indeed, it might just prove to be, literally, the Middle Path. The term itself is derived from the Buddha's finding both a life of complete indulgence and excess and a life of complete denial and asceticism to be unfulfilling in the end. Again, dualistic thinking would make us choose one or the other because science teaches you that things are either apples or oranges and never the two shall meet. The Middle Path is thus the path between two extremes.

> **KARMIC**
> # DO
> Shoveling your neighbor's walk.

> **KARMIC**
> # DON'T
> Pointing the chute of your snowblower in the direction of your neighbor's driveway.

Now that you have a broad sense of how the concept of karma evolved, we can focus on the most recognized school of thought regarding this—the Buddhist perspective.

The Buddhist Perspective

> *It is impossible to live pleasurably without living wisely, well, and justly, and impossible to live wisely, well, and justly without living pleasurably.*
>
> —Epicurus, fourth century B.C.E.

MORE THAN 2,500 YEARS AGO, in the sixth century B.C.E., while Lao Tzu and Confucius were making history in China and Pythagoras was hypnotized by the triangle in Greece, a young prince in the kingdom of what is now Nepal was about to leave his mark. His life to that point spent protectively wrapped in the sheets of luxury, at 29 he took a tour of his surroundings and was overwhelmed by the suffering and the realities of the human condition that he came into contact with.

Determined to discover both the cause of this suffering and its solution, Siddhartha Gautama left his palace, his riches, his wife, and his recently born son and embarked on a six-year journey of self-discovery

---

KARMIC DO

Watching the movie quietly.

KARMIC DON'T

Chomping popcorn and asking questions in more than a loud whisper throughout the show.

---

wandering the valley of the Ganges as an ascetic. Six years later, having learned and practiced any path promising spiritual awakening he came across, he still found himself without a sufficient explanation. One evening, completely exhausted, he sat under a tree along the bank of a river near what is now Bihar, India, and vowed to remain seated until he had found the "truth" within himself. In a blow to any of us who ever tried passing a physics test by simply staring at the textbook, Siddhartha Gautama achieved enlightenment by dawn of the following morning. He was 35. Thereafter, Gautama was known as "The Buddha," "The Enlightened One."

Karma Means Action

It's said that on the second night he spent beneath the tree, the Buddha came to an understanding of *karma*. He said that with his eyes opened, he was able to observe the way in which beings came and went, how their lives unfolded according to their karma, and how this influenced the quality of their rebirth. He borrowed the term karma, the Sanskrit word for action, from Hinduism and adjusted it to refer specifically to one's will, motivation, or intention.

We act—physically, mentally, and verbally—based on our intent or desire. The intent behind any action, its karma, inevitably shapes an action's result—its "karmic fruit," and so within each act we commit is the seed of its result. This is what is meant by "What goes around comes around." Plant an apple seed, and you'll get an apple tree—not bananas, or oranges, or a suitcase stuffed with cash. Likewise, by planting the seed of suffering, you should not be shocked when you later experience the taste of that suffering yourself. Happiness is achieved through the same means. We build up karma throughout our lives, constantly planting the seeds of our future. Since we are primarily responsible for the suffering we experience, Buddhism explains that the root cause of suffering begins in the mind, with our karma, and therefore by mastering our karma we can also foster our own happiness.

In defining karma, the Buddha used the word "volition," which means the power to choose or determine. Volition, and therefore karma, both refer to the motivation and intent behind an action. When you feel frustrated at the day's events and go home and end up taking it out on your spouse, you do so motivated by anger and the intent to harm—this is *aksula*, or unwholesome

> **KARMIC**
> # DO
> ....
> **Throwing some change in the person's cup on the sidewalk.**
>
> **KARMIC**
> # DON'T
> ....
> **Keeping the change, thinking, "He probably makes, like, 20 bucks a day."**

karma. When out of compassion and generosity you open and hold the door at the post office for a person carrying a box as big as a Volkswagen, you do so to ease their burden, and this is *kusula*, or wholesome karma. In the third grade when you put a whoopie cushion on your best friend's chair hoping others would think you were cool…well, you get the point.

Spitting in the Wind

In determining what constitutes an unwholesome act versus a wholesome act, we can look at the literal meaning of *aksula* and *kusula*. *Aksula*, or unwholesome karma, means unskillful, or not intelligent. *Kusula*, or wholesome karma, means skillful, or intelligent. We can then read these terms and what they represent as describing actions that are unintelligently committed, or committed through intention informed by wisdom. When we sit on the sofa and precariously balance a glass on the couch arm rather than the coffee table, when it falls off, breaks, and spills cranberry juice all over the white rug, this is the result of a careless decision based more on convenience and laziness than careful assessment. Indeed, a good chess player (or hustler at the pool hall) knows when to sacrifice a few pieces or games, giving his opponent the illusion of winning, only to win himself in the long run. Unwholesome acts are those committed through ignorance, ill will, and greed. Such acts will inevitably result in suffering for yourself and for others.

For example, when an automobile manufacturer tries to cut costs by skimping on the quality of paint, irate owners may notify *Consumer Reports* that their 2-year-old car looks like it's been driven on salty winter roads for 12. When a restaurant promising you the salad of the gods delivers a bowl full of iceberg lettuce and a few croutons drenched in Ranch, you'll spread the word. Like an alcoholic deceived into thinking that the bottle is his friend, we are fooled into the belief that by satisfying our karmic cravings and desires we will be happy, seeing happiness as a commodity we can purchase and as an external reward. If a retailer raises his prices and people still buy, greed may induce him to raise them still higher, at which point he'll lose business as people begin to feel they're being taken advantage of. This is karma in action.

Are All of These Your Guitars?

In 2002, David Gilmour, the guitarist for Pink Floyd, sold a house he rarely lived in and gave the money to charity. He mentioned that after a while he became bored with wealth, and that once you have six cars, you have to hire people to care for them, and then everything just gets more complicated than it's worth.

The Bottomless Pit

And still, as we witness time and time again, the more we want more, the more we will always want. The satiation of one desire only leads to another, and there is no end: Once I make $40,000, I will want $50,000. When you were six and thought you had the coolest bike on the block and felt on top of the world, you became distraught and wondered how things could be so unfair when some other kid rode by with a more expensive bike. It is never enough, and we live our lives as slaves to that which we crave.

Just What the Buddha-Doctor Ordered

While sitting under that tree, the Buddha realized that the source of human suffering was desire, dreams of ambition, a rejection of impermanence, and false hopes—all things that drive the creation of karma. To ease our suffering, it was apparent to him that we must regain control over our desires—and our addiction to fulfilling them—regardless of their impact, and to thus change our karma. As mentioned earlier, ignorance is to blame. It was ignorance that let the retailer think he could continue to raise his prices, milking his customers, and still

> **KARMIC DO**
> ....
> Cheering for your team.
>
> **KARMIC DON'T**
> ....
> Pouting because you're sitting on the bench.

maintain a successful business full of good will. Likewise, you should not expect to go to a dinner party, endlessly brag about yourself, and then expect others to go home commenting on how humble and charming you were.

When the Buddha rose, his first act, other than a good stretch, was to go share his experience and newfound knowledge with a group of hermits. The Buddha explained his new take on life as similar to the way in which a physician diagnoses a patient: He first identified the source, or cause, of the condition, then stated that the sickness can be cured, and then pulled the prescription out of his bag. The Buddha described this process in the Four Noble Truths.

The Noble Truths

The First Noble Truth, *duhkha*, explains the most prominent symptom of the human condition as one of suffering or frustration, the results of our karma. We want to have it all but get bummed when we concede that our arms could never hold it all. We wish the sun would always shine on the beach and curse the powers that be when two days out of our three-day vacation is spent under an umbrella and the sunny part of the third day is spent waiting in the airport for our plane to arrive. Remember, even the Dalai Lama catches colds, and even

Martha Stewart occasionally has a messy kitchen.

The Second Noble Truth, *trishna*, further explains the cause of suffering as being due to our refusal to accept the first noble truth, and so we continue to cling to the delusion that we can somehow alter the facts of life. A friend of mine in college was well aware that he had to fulfill his foreign language requirement to graduate. Avoiding it for as long as he could, he waited until the first semester of his senior year to deal with it. Not only did he dread the fact that the moment would eventually come, once it did, the only language he could take and complete in two semesters was Latin. Imagine the horror. Remember: Deadlines arrive, batteries die, milk

Little White Lies

A man's wife sent him to buy bread. When he got there, there was a line stretching out the door. Arriving at a story he thought would free the place up, he suddenly shouted, "Hey, the Sultan's daughter is about to be married and in honor he is giving out free bread!" The crowd quickly dispersed, and he found himself at the front of the line. At this point he realized that the Sultan was giving out free bread while he was in line to pay for some, so he ran to the palace, where he was beaten by an angry and breadless crowd.

Moral of the story: When we routinely deceive others, we often end up believing our own lies.

spoils, we get older and our health deteriorates, vacations end, pets pass away, flowers wilt, sensations of "victory!" pass—"Life's a bitch," the Buddha could have said (though he probably didn't). Buddhists refer to this sea of

sorrow as *samsara*, an endless cycle of birth, death, and rebirth, powered by that ceaseless chain of cause and effect—karma.

The Third Noble Truth states that there is a way to transcend this suffering and to lead a life of happiness—there is, in fact, a pot of gold at the end of the rainbow, we just have to get there. We can be released

from the endless cycle of *samsara*. It's like hitting the jackpot on the slot machines not because of luck, fate, or divine intervention (more on this in the next section), but because we simply played our cards right. Remember: You can't hit the proverbial jackpot if you don't play the game. The Fourth Noble Truth explains the "prescription" for attaining Buddhahood and therefore *nirvana*. It is the Eightfold Path, commonly referred to as "The Middle Path," which leads to the cessation of suffering, or *duhkha*. We'll come back to the Eightfold Path in Chapter 3.

> **KARMIC**
> # DO
> ....
> **Giving an elderly person your seat on a bus.**
>
> **KARMIC**
> # DON'T
> ....
> **Racing a guy on crutches to a taxi.**

Debunking Karmic Myths

It is not...karma that rewards or punishes us,
but it is we who punish and reward ourselves.

—H. P. Blavatsky, founder of the
Theosophical Society

BECAUSE OF ITS ASSOCIATION WITH BUDDHISM and Hinduism, karma is often misinterpreted in the West as being a religious law of morality. But karma has nothing to do with moral judgment or divine intervention. It is, pure and simple, a natural law of cause and effect: You do something and there is a result. Something happens and there is a cause. You kick the wall and you stub your toe. You smile and you make someone happy. Karma is neutral—we are the ones that judge the outcome as good or bad. Karma is also not to be confused with fate or destiny.

We *Can* Change Our Karma

Both fate and destiny assume things are moving toward an outcome that is inevitable and cannot be changed. "I'm destined to be great," a child prodigy might boast to her classmates, but if she spends most of her time debating the finer points of rationalism with her peers, she may only get a reputation for being argumentative. Karma is more about potential—the six-year-old child with the violin skills of a virtuoso has the *potential* to become great—but it is not predetermined, and we must actively choose to make it so. Karma can always be changed; fate or destiny cannot. Karma, then, is the complete opposite of fate or destiny.

We are constantly in the act of creating karma and always have within us the power to change what we do now in order to affect the future. As owners of our own karma, we also own the end result: You broke it, you bought it. Karma is also a complete disavowal of the idea of heaven or hell because each of those suggests that once we've entered either, we exist within an eternal state of punishment or an eternal state of reward. Karma can always be changed. To this end, karma is not the product of divine intervention, as there is no intervention other than our own and that of others. Like the potent smell of sour milk, the truth of karma is simply an inherent aspect of the universe itself.

The Problem of "Whodunnit"

Take the idea of any occurrence that happens seemingly unexpectedly. It could be anything: a car accident, winning a raffle, getting a flat tire, getting a zit the night before the prom, buying a $200 dress a day before it goes on sale for $75. While we might explain any of them away as the result of mere chance, coincidence, good or bad luck, fate, or perhaps even God's will, the important thing to realize is that all of these explanations suggest we had no control over the events, that they were caused by either divine intervention or statistical randomness.

Chance, Coincidence, and Karma

These two terms—chance and coincidence—are tossed around so often we've come to accept them as almost concrete explanations. But look at what the words actually mean. They suggest that whatever just happened was completely random: It just, well, happened. Chance is somewhat like luck—the result of a roll of the dice, or the words that come up when you give your Magic Eight Ball a good shake and ask it a question. Coincidence suggests that a couple of things in the universe aligned and caused something to happen that is so rare and unpredictable, you should just throw your hands up in the air with a sigh or whip out your astrology book to see if Mercury was just in retrograde.

But if an event is so rare and unpredictable, how did it happen? Coincidence? Well, not exactly. If it happened it happened. Science tells us that there is a cause for everything, we accept that rule, and then the moment something happens that surprises us we suddenly revert to complete superstition in the modern sense, believing in such things as luck, chance, and coincidence.

Because of their belief in karma, Buddhists don't believe in chance and coincidence—though events unfold due to the interaction of innumerable variables, and there is a "cause" or a "because" for everything. The chance meeting you had the other day when you bumped into an old friend as you walked out of the bank and whom you hadn't seen in years was not an accident, but that doesn't mean it was fate, either. Instead, it can be explained as the sum results of all of your previous actions and your impulses at the current moment. Your karma—when mixed with that of your friend—brought the situation to fruition.

> **KARMIC**
> # DO
> ....
> **Replacing the empty roll of toilet paper.**
>
> **KARMIC**
> # DON'T
> ....
> **Putting the empty orange juice container back in the fridge.**

The Issue of "What If?"

A family going on a road trip gets an hour into the drive when they discover they forgot the keys to their vacation house. They turn around amid a few groans to go back and get them. Keys in hand, they set off once again. Forty-five minutes later they realize they forgot one of the suitcases,

Religion, Science, Dogma, and Fear of the Truth

When Copernicus believed that the Earth revolved around the sun rather than vice versa, he was afraid to publish his thoughts out of fear of the Church. On his deathbed, it's said he uttered the words, "No matter what they say, the Earth revolves around the sun." One hundred years later, Galileo proved him right.

which holds the camera, towels, bathing suits, and the gift they were going to leave for their friend. Again, they turn around. Now, three hours later, they are setting off again. When they reach the point at which they last had to turn around, they find a massive pileup of cars in disarray surrounding an 18-wheeler that jackknifed on the highway.

"Wow, we could have been in that if we hadn't had to go back to pick up the keys and then the suitcase...what karma," they might say. "Imagine if we'd been here an hour or two earlier." When they tell a few of their more skeptical friends, they may be met with "karma dismissal," as their friends explain that it was, of course, just chance or coincidence. It's often the case that when we deny the existence of fate or predestination, we assume that our only other option is to assume the rule of chance and coincidence.

But if the events are looked at in the framework of an

organic whole in which everything affects everything, a different picture emerges that suggests karma *did* certainly play a role, but there was nothing divine about it. Remember that karma refers to volition or intent, which then drive our actions, which then have effects or results. The family wished to go on a vacation and so they set the process in motion. In each moment, they were faced with choices that would alter each moment.

They could have continued on without the keys because the idea of going back was too much of a pain and they assumed they would figure a way in once they got there. If they had continued, their very presence would have altered the unfolding day, and there is no way to say the truck would still have jack-knifed. Instead of taking the risk, the family decided to go back and get the keys. When they realized they'd forgotten the suitcase, they were again faced with several options. The point of all of this is that there is no way to prove fate or destiny; the only thing one can say is that things happen along with the choices that we make—we can only know what happens *when* it happens. In this way, our karma is an inherent

KARMIC DO

Picking up after your dog.

KARMIC DON'T

Looking the other way doing your best take, "What dog? My dog? Never seen him before."

aspect of our lives and the lives of others. There's really nothing mystical about it.

Gods, Religion, and Karma

We live in an age of skepticism and tend not to accept anything on blind faith—most of us knew Milli Vanilli weren't singing, didn't expect to really make $1,500 to $5,000 working from home when we called the number posted on the telephone pole, knew that we weren't an instant $12 million dollar winner even though the envelope we got in the mail said we were—and we follow the scientific principal that for something to exist we must be able to see it in action. Furthermore, if it happened once, we believe it should be able to happen again.

For this reason, many have dismissed traditional organized religion as somewhat of a hocus-pocus kind of archaic mysticism used to explain the universe before the advent of science, and see the Bible as historical analogies similar to Greek myths. Jonah couldn't have been swallowed by a whale and survived in the belly of the beast to once again roam the earth because that's ridiculous (only slightly more plausible would be the idea that he was eaten by one). If Noah had actually taken a pair of each species of animal on his ark, wouldn't the gazelle have been a goner keeping such close company with a lion?

Did he quickly make a trip over to South America, picking up two giant anteaters plus enough ants to keep them both happy? Imagine if the male had been impotent…No, if anything, most of us have grown to see both the Old and New Testament as the grandest of folk tales, and as epics of their times.

Organized religion is premised on the notion of an omnipotent and supreme being, a sentient being, with jurisdiction over the universe. In this way, many seek solace in the knowledge that criminals will get their due, and the righteous theirs. But the Buddha did not consider himself a god, deity, or anything more than human. Though he is almost always referred to as "The Buddha," the term itself is not reserved for him alone. Anyone can be a Buddha, and every individual has within the potential to become one. We must simply free ourselves from delusions of grandeur and act with love and wisdom.

KARMIC DO

Attempting to nurse a sick goldfish back to health.

KARMIC DON'T

Flushing the fish.

Karma's Arrival in the West

And so our mothers and grandmothers have, more often than not anonymously, handed on the creative spark, the seed of the flower they themselves never hoped to see — or like a sealed letter they could not plainly read.

—Alice Walker

REGARDLESS OF HOW WELL it is understood, karma is everywhere these days. "My karma ran over my dogma" adorns the rear bumper of an endless number of Volvo wagons; Radiohead sings an ode to the term in "Karma Police;" ask a fifth-grader about the term and even if you don't get a specific definition, you'll most likely get a nod of recognition. The term regularly pops up in cartoons, movies, contemporary literature, and even the dictionary. I've even heard a basketball announcer scream, "Now that is karmic basketball!" after a dramatic final-four game.

So how and when did the term make its debut in the West? Karma never made a solo journey across the ocean, but like the fortune in the cookie or the worm in the tequila, karma came already embedded within a theology and philosophy. While the Beatles may have made Eastern thought popular here in the late 60s, the initial stirrings began much earlier.

While Indian philosophy began making its way west in the fourth century B.C.E., when Alexander the Great came to India with an entourage of scientists, artists, and historians, Buddhism was slowly spreading throughout Asia, making its way to China by the first century C.E. and landing in Japan by 550 C.E. But for almost another thousand years, the West would view the East, or the Orient, as it was known at the time, as little more than exotic and mystical.

Coming to America

In the nineteenth century the United States came face to face with the East, and it happened through gold. The gold rush drew 20,000 Chinese immigrants to California and, by 1860, one out of ten Californians was Chinese. Soon, San Francisco had its first Chinese temple in Chinatown. By the close of the nineteenth century, there were more than 400 temples on the West Coast. The religion the immigrants brought with them was a mix of Confucianism, Taoism, and Buddhism. Though at first welcomed as laborers, sentiment soon changed to resentment. America was experiencing a fundamentalist revival, and general attempts to convert the Chinese were met with frustration. One missionary went so far as to explain that Taoism, Buddhism, opium addiction, and ancestor worship comprised the four elements of paganism.

From the early 1900s until the present there is a somewhat tangled, yet beautiful, progression of Eastern thought making its way into American popular culture. In 1893, the World Parliament of Religions was held in Chicago on the shores of Lake Michigan. In a show of comparative theology, it was a gathering of religions running the spectrum from Christianity to non-Christian Asian religions. Christians argued that Buddhism, positing no sole creator and no soul, could not educate people as to the issues of personal sin and also left the future a dark and scary unknown. In their turn, Buddhists argued that Buddhism, because it posited no God or creator and mentioned no miracles, offered a bridge between religion and science. One of the Buddhist speakers, Soyen Shaku, spoke on the topic of cause and effect—otherwise known as karma—as understood by the Buddha.

Bring in the Beats

In first half of the twentieth century, writers such as Thoreau, Emerson, and Huxley were incorporating bits of Eastern philosophy into their writings; Emerson wrote an essay on the nature of compensation, explaining the natural law of karma as a force that invariably sought to bring events, people, and the universe into a balanced harmony—when someone dies another is born; when a bough of a tree is bent it attempts to return to its previous angle; when Angelina Jolie gets a tattoo, she inevitably begins the process of once again planning a new tattoo; and unfortunately, when an annoying person becomes momentarily pleasant, they inevitably begin working their way back again to becoming annoying—such is life, such is karma.

> **KARMIC**
> # DO
> ....
> **Helping a friend move her grand piano up five flights of stairs.**
>
> **KARMIC**
> # DON'T
> ....
> **Pretending you're busy on moving day.**

In the mid-1940s Allen Ginsberg, Neal Cassady, and Jack Kerouac, three fathers of the burgeoning Beat Generation, were attending Columbia University together and became friends. In 1953, Allen Ginsberg, who had become interested in Buddhism, showed up at the door of the First Zen Institute in New York City. He found the place a bit intimidating and didn't stay long, but wrote Neal Cassady, now in California, to tell him of his new interests. At the time, Jack Kerouac also discovered Buddhism and Hindu philosophy while reading Thoreau. He had been depressed and was thinking that he might follow in Thoreau's footsteps and go live in the woods. Shortly afterward, he kind of did.

Kerouac moved in with his sister and spent his days chopping wood and his nights writing three books on Buddhism, *Some of the Dharma, Wake Up,* and *Buddha Tells Us.* Eventually he would write the wildly popular *Dharma Bums* (in ten nights at his mother's house) in which he chronicled the Buddhist escapades of himself, Ginsberg, Cassady, and Gary Snyder (a Zen poet and friend of Ginsberg, Cassady, and Kerouac who largely inspired Kerouac to write the book). In 1955, Ginsberg went public with his epic poem *Howl* at the Sixth Street Gallery in San Francisco, and this marked the beginning of what would become known as the "San Francisco Renaissance," and the foundation for the upcoming American Zen Boom was set.

KARMIC
DO
....
Saying "Hi" and making eye contact with the cashier who's ringing you up.

KARMIC
DON'T
....
Ignoring the sales clerk.

The San Francisco Scene

While the Zen Boom of the late 1950s was marked by intellectual discussions and the Buddhist-inspired poetry and writings of the Beat Generation (a term coined by Kerouac, as the term "beat" seemed to sum up the way he felt) taking place in coffeehouses and cocktail parties, with the 60s, things began to change. Buddhism, Zen Buddhism, and Hinduism exploded into the free-spirited and experimental culture that began to blossom. Drugs, discontent with the Vietnam War, the ensuing peace movement, the civil rights movement, and the immigration to the West of Tibetan Buddhists after the Chinese invasion of Tibet in 1959 combined in a powerful dynamic, pushing Eastern culture to the forefront of the Western conscience.

The San Francisco Zen Center was just around the corner from the scene at Haight-Ashbury. Timothy Leary was making the rounds with his rowdy group of LSD-ingesting hippies, the Merry Pranksters (of which Neal Cassady was one of the more celebrated members), and hallucinogenics seemed conducive to the appreciation of images of surreal Hindu deities ("Just look at that six-armed blue-guy"). Gary Snyder read poetry at the Filmore from a lotus position; the American Buddhist and writer Alan Watts was lecturing to crowds of more than 500 at the Avalon Ballroom (where there was even a "Zenefit" featuring the Grateful Dead, Big Brother and the Holding Company, and Quicksilver Messenger Service).

Members of the koka-an Zendo in San Francisco, surprised at growing attendance, had the question answered when they learned word had gotten out that the

Please, Won't You Be My Guru?

While on the way to a party celebrating the publication of his book *Dharma Bums*, Jack Kerouac hopped into a phone booth and called D. T. Suzuki, one of the first Zen teachers in the United States, to ask him if he and his friends, Allen Ginsberg and Peter Orlovsky, could stop by for a visit. When Suzuki asked him when, Kerouac hollered, "Right now!" And so they went. Suzuki sat them down and told them to sit quietly and to write haikus while he made some green tea. On their way out afterward, Kerouac said, "I would like to spend the rest of my life with you," to which Suzuki replied rather noncommittally, "Sometime."

koka-an Zendo was a great place to trip. In 1962, Allen Ginsberg, Gary Snyder, and Peter Orlovsky (a poet and Ginsberg's lover) went to India. One of Ginsberg's goals was to find a method to try and keep his own ego in check. The eyes, as well as many of the bodies, of the counterculture followed.

Indian Gurus and Some Beatles

In 1965, the Beatles were in India on the set of their movie *Help*. George Harrison fell in love with the sitar and returned in 1966 to study the instrument under Ravi Shankar. In 1967 Harrison, John Lennon, Ringo Starr, and Paul McCartney took up residence in Rishikesh, India, studying transcendental meditation under

Maharishi Mahesh Yogi, introduced to them by Harrison's wife, Patty. Ringo and his wife stayed a little less than two weeks, and while the others stayed on, things turned sour. They began to see the Maharishi as corrupt and living a life of double standards. Though he insisted on a diet of no meat for his "disciples," they soon discovered that the Maharishi was smuggling in chicken for himself. John Lennon wrote "Sexy Sadie" about the Maharishi, singing, "Sexy Sadie what have you done / you've made a fool of everyone."

Nevertheless, cultural transmission had taken place, and despite their experience with the Maharishi, the Beatles embraced the lessons of the East. Two years after "Sexy Sadie," Lennon came out with "Instant Karma," this time announcing, "Instant Karma's gonna get you / gonna knock you off your feet." In 1970 George Harrison put out "My Sweet Lord," in which he chants "hare krishna." The die had been cast, everyone wanted an Indian guru, and karma was cool.

The Counterculture Embraces the East

The counterculture ushered in drugs, music, and Eastern philosophy: Astrology was hip and people were consulting their chakras, looking for gurus, and searching for deeper levels of spirituality. Capitalism was seen as an evil, Martin Luther King and Gandhi were cultural heroes, and the youth were encouraged to tune in, drop out, and search for peace. Things were "heavy," "vibes" ruled the universe, and there was a convenient aspect of Eastern philosophy to parallel all of this: karma. "Dude, that's some heavy karma;" "That was so karmic;" "Ooh, bad karma, man." Karma was cool, associated with images of Indian holy men with long hair and no belongings who seemed to have it "all figured out" roaming in the nude while smoking hashish during the Summer of Love.

Mind expansion was the name of the game, in direct opposition to the established Western status quo, which had determined all but the West to be primitive and uncivilized and Christ to be at the helm of the ship. God is good, but then God was dead. Head to India. While the Beatles may have paved the way and the Beat poets and intellectuals opened the door, those who followed came to escape. The West's emphasis on the individual and capitalism became synonymous with ego and greed. Hippies flocked to escape and find their souls.

> **KARMIC DO**
> ....
> Calling someone you know would like to hear from you.

> **KARMIC DON'T**
> ....
> Leaving it, thinking you can always do it later.

At the 1968 Democratic National Convention in Chicago, Allen Ginsberg was among the crowd protesting the U.S. involvement in the Vietnam War. He chanted "OM" from a mike on the stage in an attempt to calm the crowd as the police moved in with tear gas and billy clubs. Eastern philosophy had met Western popular culture headfirst. And as Indian writer Gita Mehta would later comment, in exchange for karma the West gave the Eastern world Coca-Cola. No doubt, "My karma ran over my dogma."

Counterculture Becomes Popular Culture

As with any cultural process or change, if something new takes hold, it soon shifts from representing counterculture to representing popular culture. Grunge was considered alternative until it became so well accepted that it could be called normal. Men with long hair could call themselves rebels until fashion models began sporting the look.

Karma and the philosophy it came from were no different. Though the time existed when if you yelled "Karma!" on the street someone might scream back, "Karma who?!" or if you wanted the word "karma" to appear on your VW bus you'd have to spray-paint it on, by the 1980s people on the street knew what you were talking about and you could just buy the bumper sticker.

By the 1990s karma was as embedded in Western culture as the infomercial, and in the twenty-first century, it's become the ultimate marketing darling. Add the word karma to anything and you've injected it with the exotic.

Heart of Gold

IN THE LATE 1960s AND 70s, Neil Young secured his status both on his own and in bands like Buffalo Springfield and Crosby, Stills, Nash, and Young. In the early 80s, he was wooed from his label, Reprise records, by David Geffen. Geffen offered him $3 million less than another company, but lured him with the promise that Young would have complete artistic control and could make whatever kinds of albums he wanted—without commercial pressure. Neil Young took him up on the offer, literally, and churned out several experimental albums. He released *Trans*, on which he sang with his voice put through computerized vocoder; *Everybody's Rockin'*, which was composed of rockabilly tunes; *Old Ways,* which featured Willie Nelson and Waylon Jennings; *Landing on Water,* which was full of synthesizers—all albums that diverged heavily from the stuff that had made him famous. None of them sold well, and David Geffen sued him for $3 million for making "unrepresentative" and noncommercial music. Neil Young countersued for $21 million; eventually, both suits were dropped and

> **KARMIC**
> # DO
> **Putting yourself in someone else's shoes.**
>
> **KARMIC**
> # DON'T
> **Trying on pants in a clothing store without underwear.**

Neil Young went back to Reprise Records and dove back into the arms of popular culture.

Moral of the story: Like Geffen, we should be careful what we ask for—'cause we might just get it. You break it, you buy it. It's karma.

CHAPTER 2

How Does Karma Work?

Somebody once said we never know what is
enough until we know what's more than enough.

—Billie Holiday

CASE STUDY
Zen and the Art of Moving Trucks

TIM WAS A DRIVER for a moving company. Occasionally his boss let him use one of the moving trucks for his own transportation. As an added bonus, Tim also discovered that when things weren't going so well with his girlfriend, the back of the truck also made for a convenient—if dark—studio apartment.

Tim's sister owned several acres of wooded land filled with old logging roads. With the innate intelligence characteristic of folks easily seduced by the potential for disaster, Tim decided to take the moving truck there one cold, snowy day in the dead of winter and became hopelessly stuck. He tried frantically to get the truck out, but his 6'2" frame and 190 pounds were no match for an entrenched moving truck. For some inexplicable reason, Tim happened to have a camcorder with him. Awed at the ridiculousness of the situation, he decided to tape the ordeal for the sake of posterity.

He hitched a ride back to town to try and round up a few friends to help him. Tim showed the video to his girlfriend, then left with his buddies to get the truck. A few minutes later, his boss stopped by his house to find out where Tim and the truck were. His girlfriend innocently played the tape to an incredulous boss.

Moral of the story: We usually know what's coming, yet we ignore it at our own peril.

Karma. Because It's the Law

Karma is the web of life, the total pattern of cause and effect.

—Clarence Pedersen, in *The Source of Becauses*

KARMA CAN SEEM LIKE AN ABSTRACT and completely unobservable phenomenon when it's talked about in the context of cycles of death and rebirth. For most of us, traveling in the fast lane of the twenty-first century, it would seem there are more pressing issues than spending a lot of time debating issues of the next life and how to reach nirvana.

But in our homes and offices, we *can* observe the behavior of karma in each and every moment. Both Hindus and Buddhists consider karma a natural law, and it is often compared to Isaac Newton's laws of motion.

Assuming you paid about as much attention during physics as I did, here's a quick review. Newton's first law of motion states that if no forces are present, an object at rest will stay at rest, and an object moving at a constant velocity in a straight line will do so indefinitely. His second law explains that when a force is exerted on an object, the object will accelerate, and the acceleration will be in the direction of the force and proportional in strength to the force, and inversely proportional to the object's mass (essentially, the force will have to overcome the weight of the object if the object is to be moved). The third law says, "To every action there is an equal and opposite reaction." Indeed, what goes up must come down.

With our bodies as the object, and our will, or karma, the force, we can navigate the course of our own lives according to these laws. At birth, we initially inhabit a body that is at rest. As desire and sensory perception develop, we start creating karma as we attempt to satisfy our wants and needs, building momentum in the process.

Monumental Momentum

Imagine a teenage girl who decides that she wants to be a doctor. As time passes, she increasingly dedicates herself to that direction: She studies hard to get good grades, so that she can get into a good med school, so that she can eventually realize her goal of becoming a physician. Although much of this may be unconscious, most of what she does while she's growing up is to get nearer to this goal. This is her karma and, like raindrops to a stream, each karmic act she commits, no matter how small, increases the force with which she moves in a particular direction. When she enters med school, she does so on the momentum she has created over the course of her life up until that point. Her karma never sealed her fate or created her destiny to be a doctor, it only increased the probability and helped create the path. So she becomes a physician, and perhaps over time she begins to lose interest. The force and momentum she has built up support her life as a doctor and, at this point, like a gear on a well-oiled track, her life has become like a routine. Now

> **KARMIC**
> # DO
> ....
> **Bringing enough to share.**
>
> **KARMIC**
> # DON'T
> ....
> **Assuming someone else will.**

dissatisfied, she ponders taking another direction and is faced with finding the energy required to change—the force required to change her karma.

Like Stopping a Train?

There are bills to keep up with, relationships she's developed, and a lifestyle that has developed a momentum of its own. It seems like the same amount of effort that went into getting things rolling to begin with is now required to change it—an opposite push of the same force. After much frustration and effort, she may finally stop the "ball" she started rolling all those years ago, and is now free to move in a new direction. In Buddhism this is known as working through our karma.

Whatever our goal, we have all experienced the feeling of commitment, of starting to get in deep where it would take longer to get back than to go forth. Think of a recent car trip where you were a bit ambivalent about whether you should go. Once that halfway point has been reached, the momentum is easier to ride than to stop, and you think, "Well, I've come this far, I might as well keep going."

Every Action Has a Reaction

For Newton's third law of motion, think of a cannon shooting a cannonball. When the cannon is shot, the source experiences recoil, equal to the force that was used to fire the ball. We fully expect this, are not surprised by it, and would be puzzled if there were no repercussion after committing such an action. Karma is automatic: There is no intervening time period in which the action is assessed, judgment made, and result caused. We expect that every action occasions a result.

Thoughts Are Actions

The difference between the law of karma and Newton's laws of motion lies in scope. As was considered scientific at the time, there was nothing but matter in the world: That which you cannot see does not exist. This approach considered feelings, thoughts, emotions, and spiritual experiences to be flights of fancy and irrelevant to the "real" world. But there is actually another intriguing parallel between karma and Newtonian mechanics. Though he wished to have a system based solely on observables, Newton had a problem. While an apple can be seen to fall out of a tree and land on somebody's head, there is nothing visible you can see that makes it fall. Newton was forced to make an assumption; without it, his theories would fall flat. The assumption he made was gravity: You can't see it, but something is obviously making that apple fall. The only proof that gravity exists is by witnessing its effects. Karma is quite similar. Karma is, however, much more far-reaching, and while it explains the behaviors of forces and matter, it can also account for those of life, consciousness, and purpose of intent.

KARMIC
DO

Letting the person behind you, who is buying only cough syrup, go first.

KARMIC
DON'T

Cruising through the express "10 items or less, cash only" lane with 19 items and paying with a check.

It's All about Cause and Effect

They paved paradise, and put up a parking lot.

—Joni Mitchell, in "Big Yellow Taxi," 1969

CAUSE AND EFFECT are not always so easy to break down into "This directly caused that." Our lives do not take place in a vacuum, for we are in constant interaction with everything and everyone. Karma is reflective of an organic, as opposed to a mechanical, universe. Think of karma as analogous to interacting weather patterns.

Playing the Blame Game

Consider the following: You're walking down an icy sidewalk one morning. You slip, fall, and experience the pain of a bruised tailbone. Frustrated, you pound the ice with your fist for its blatant transgression against you. Rubbing your hand, you look at the house you're currently sitting in front of and notice a man getting into his car on his way to work. "Idiot," you think, "why didn't he just shovel his walk?"

Is it his fault? Perhaps normally he does shovel his walk, but on this particular morning he overslept because his infant son had been up the entire night with a fever.

Is it the baby's fault? Perhaps the infant became ill from coming into contact with another child. When trying to trace cause and effect back, it becomes impossible to identify a specific cause that started it all—and then you can only say, "Damn the universe for existing, because if it didn't, I wouldn't have fallen on this ice." Each and every person is constantly creating and experiencing karma, and affecting others in an interdependent relationship.

Einstein and the Buddha

The analogies between science and karma do not stop with Newton. Newton had a problem: If everything has a cause that preceded it, what is responsible for the "thing" that starts something in the first place? Newton was a religious man and satisfied himself with answering, "God." Buddhism answers the question with a theory drawn from modern physics—in this case, Einstein and his theory of relativity.

Imagine three friends, each of whom has his own spaceship, approaching three satellites from three different directions. They are then to determine which satellite blinks first, unaware that the satellites have been set to

> **KARMIC DO**
> Moving a turtle out of the road.
>
> **KARMIC DON'T**
> Driving by, thinking, "Bummer to be the turtle."

blink simultaneously. Each will perceive a different satellite to blink first, then second, then third. Because the light from the satellite farthest from you takes longer to reach you, the closest one to you will appear to blink before the others. Who is right? According to Einstein, each is right, from his own perspective. It is the same with karma—all that can be said is that things are in interaction and together contribute to the whole. Isolating one factor can never explain what follows.

Instant Karma, Instant Change

Linear time and Newtonian mechanics show a direct link between cause and effect that are tied together consecutively—this happened, then this happened, then this happened, and here is the result of all those happenings. But what this does not allow is anything to happen simultaneously, and this limits our ability to understand certain events because we assume that they must fit our model. During the 1970s, DC-10s seemed to be crashing quicker than bugs on a windshield. To discover the cause and fix the problem, investigators broke down all the events that led up to the mechanical failure. They put it on a timeline: First this failed, which caused that to go, which then made this happen. By tracing it back, they determined that there was one faulty piece creating a chain

Buddhist Theory of Relativity

The Buddha mulled over the following factors and concluded that they were all interdependent. As suffering is caused by ignorance, desire, and clinging, he reasoned happiness was achieved by eliminating them.

- Ignorance fosters the conditioning of karma.
- Through these actions of karma we condition consciousness.
- Consciousness conditions mental and physical phenomena.
- With mental and physical phenomena our five sense organs and mind are conditioned.
- Through these six (sense organs and mind), contact is conditioned.
- Sensorial and mental contact condition sensation.
- Through sensation desire and craving are conditioned.
- Craving and desire condition clinging, or attachment.
- Clinging conditions becoming.
- Becoming conditions birth.
- Birth conditions pain, suffering, decay, and death.

reaction of failure. It was one bolt. They thought the solution then was simple: Redesign the bolt. But later it was discovered that it was not, in fact, the bolt that set the whole process in motion. Several interdependent mechanical parts in the plane, of which the bolt was one, had in actuality all failed simultaneously. As we see the universe as a unified whole, a change in one part creates a change in the whole, and the order of these changes will be relative to wherever you are.

The Quantum Karmic Connection

The really interesting thing has been to see how modern science from the time of Einstein has come full circle back to the perspective of the universe as an organic whole in which everything is interdependent, and cause and effect are no longer dominated by linear notions of space and time. Science may have now solved that thorn every scientist would love to pluck out of their side: action at a distance, or the question of, "How can 'objects' that appear to have no physical contact with each other affect each other?"

Quantum physics took the concept of the universe as separated by time and space—and that no change can take place faster than the speed of light—and flipped it on its head. Now, interactions and effects can be instantaneous regardless of distance. It was discovered that particles that were once part of a "single" system of interaction will continue to act and react together regardless of how they are later separated.

The true implications of this become apparent when we consider that the universe as we know it originated in the Big Bang, from one point, and so now every particle in every galaxy is intimately related to the others; instead of a simple mechanistic view, we must now take a holistic view of an organic universe. So, while that reenactment you watched the other night on TV might have sent a giggle through everyone in the room, truth is, when a woman in Denver burned her arm on a skillet while making scrambled eggs for her kids, her mother in Wisconsin *may* have felt a tingling sensation in her forearm. A horribly "unscientific" situation, but modern physics would allow for it. Now, whether that spot on *Ripley's Believe It or Not* really happened is another story.

If Not Now, When? Where's My Karma?

Notions of karma can often seem elusive or abstract because the karmic fruit of an action doesn't always show up immediately. When we think of cause and effect, we often think of things such as flipping a light switch and the light comes on, or swinging a hammer, which hits a nail, and the force of the hit causes the nail to go in. But in Eastern conceptions of karma, some effects are believed not to show up for several lifetimes. A parallel for this can be seen in genetics. A grandmother may be a carrier for a specific trait, yet it may not show itself in a descendent for several generations. Another example is pollution. We are only now seeing some of the effects to the planet caused by industrialization. On the other hand, if karma worked more like receiving an electric shock immediately after committing a negative act and was then over, our behavior would be more akin to a dog that won't run through his invisible fence. And where's the fun in that?

Individual, Collective, and Universal Karma

Three passions, simple but overwhelmingly strong, have governed my life: the longing for love, the search for knowledge, and unbearable pity for the suffering of mankind.

—Bertrand Russell, Nobel Prize–winning author, in his 1967 autobiography

WHILE THE CLASSIC NOTION of karma takes place on the personal level, because of the basic interdependence that exists, everybody's karma is in constant interaction with everybody else's karma. As a result, we are affected by not only our own karma but the karma of others as well. When there's a meeting at work and two or three people invariably show up late, the mood can be significantly altered. This is collective karma.

When individual and collective karma are combined, we arrive at the karma of the universe. Again, consider the interactions of karma as similar to weather patterns: What goes around comes around. It is therefore in our best interest to create good karma—when it rains in

Ohio, a day or so later upstate New York experiences the same. In good Buddhist fashion, because cause and effect are relative, one cannot say whether universal karma causes individual karma or vice versa—all that really can be said is that they interact, are interdependent, and cause each other. Sit in a traffic jam at rush hour during a rainstorm and you're experiencing a mixture of collective, universal, and individual karma.

Your Very Own Karma

Individual karma is your own gig, the consequences of all you've done and all you do. As karma comes from the Sanskrit word for "action," you are the sum total of your actions and therefore the sum total of your karma.

> **KARMIC**
> # DO
> ....
> **Bringing your library books back on time.**
>
> **KARMIC**
> # DON'T
> ....
> **Leaving library VHS tapes on your car dash in the hot sun.**

Buddhism proposes that you are the result of five aggregates: matter, sensations, perceptions, mental formations, and consciousness. The interaction of these five aggregates combine to form your sense of "I." Therefore, you are your own karma.

Think of how your friends know you. They know you through your karma: what you've done in the past, what you're doing now, the things you're planning for the future. Indeed, your karma precedes you. When you go to meet some friends for dinner and they introduce you to some of their friends, they do so by describing your path—or your karma: "Oh, Jane's a case worker at Family and Children's Service and she's been…"

We Are Our Own Closets

Buddhism would propose that you remain "you" based on your desire to be "you." 'Tis the brave soul who will subdue the ego in favor of the common good, but it is also the wise soul. Through our desire to "be," we accumulate things: money, partners, commercial goods, Pez dispensers from e-bay, stamp collections from your uncle Mort. Through attraction to these things, we then define ourselves, ask others to see us in the same way, and try to maintain a stable sense of self—granted, sometimes we're more convincing than other times. If you say you're a guitarist, it follows that you'll play the guitar every now and then in order for the label to make sense. If you say you're a vegetarian, most likely you won't order the filet mignon. If you say you're a Trekkie…well, maybe you shouldn't.

Your Karma in Harmony

Even when you act in a manner that is true to yourself,

you may still be upsetting the balance of nature around you. Maintaining a relative sense of you is important, for where certain behavior may seem balanced in certain situations, the same behavior can seem out of whack in another setting. For example, lecturing a group of people on the hazards of airplane travel can be a useful discussion at dinner; lecturing a group of passengers waiting in Terminal B14 about the potential for disaster serves only to put everyone on edge. While explaining to some friends a number of reasons you think a certain couple might not be the best for each other in the initial stages of their relationship might be instructive; doing so at the head table during their wedding can backfire.

Collective, or Group, Karma

Although karma has consequences for the individual and we are responsible for our own karma, karma itself is not an individual law but a law of the universe. Just as we experience gravity and it affects us differently depending whether we've just jumped off a swing or are sitting on the ground and having a picnic, we are all experiencing its effects.

Consider a team sport like basketball or football. The karma, or intent, of each player on one team combines in each moment with the karma and intent of each player on the other team, and it is this combination that creates the game and determines its direction. People who are depressed don't play as well, people who don't care don't

play as well, and these attitudes affect the attitudes of the players, for better or for worse. Looking at it this way, karma is not so much mystical as it is an explanation of group dynamics. There are no moral judgments being handed out, only the reality of people interacting.

We see the result of collective, or group, karma all the time. At parties, in meetings, at home, on Capital

> **KARMIC**
> # DO
> ....
> **Locking your car doors and removing your valuables.**
>
> **KARMIC**
> # DON'T
> ....
> **Installing a car alarm that will go off if as much as a ladybug lands on the hood.**

Hill, on *Oprah,* on MTV's *The Real World*. Some of the more interesting instances happen at a singles party. Everyone is trying to impress everyone else, deception flies around the room, karmas mix like a tie-dye, and you never know what will come of it or where you'll find yourself within it.

The Universe and One Huge Vat of Karmic Soup

We are all part of an organic whole. As with the Buddhist law of dependent origination, there is no single karmic act that is solely responsible for all others. The karma of the universe is both a result of individual and collective karma, *and* the cause. If we assume that the universe is a massive bowl of soup and each of us a spice or vegetable, the overall quality and taste of the soup is a result of all the interactions taking place. The spice is not the soup nor is the soup the spice. In the same way, you can think of the overall karma of the universe as the result of all the different karmas of individuals and things within it, everything being interdependent.

> ### KARMIC
> # DO
> ....
> **Paying for the car behind you at the tollbooth.**
>
> ### KARMIC
> # DON'T
> ....
> **Trying to switch lanes when no one is moving so you become a diagonal obstacle to the flow.**

Part of the difficulty for us in understanding the karma of the cosmos is that we are taught to see it as a separate entity from us. So one might ask, "Well, what is the intent of the cosmos, and how does it practice karma?" *It* practices karma because *we* practice karma. We are all ingredients, and it is up to each of us to make sure the overall taste is good.

As a never-ending chain of cause and effect, karma is inherently kept in motion by its natural tendency to continue and reproduce. The desire to "to be, to exist, to re-exist, to become more and more, to grow more and more, to accumulate more and more" serves as a good basis for the Buddhist conception of reincarnation.

Reincarnation—From the Beatles to Nirvana

I always wanted to be somebody...but I should have been more specific.

—Lily Tomlin

BEEN BAD AND WORRY you're about to come back as a tree slug in your next life? Well...you might, but the good thing is, you probably won't be aware of it. When someone mentions reincarnation, you're not alone if your mind suddenly comes alight with images of a guest on Sally Jesse Raphael's show who works as a hair stylist, loudly insisting that she was an ancient Egyptian princess in a past life so there's no way in hell she's gotta stand there and let anyone talk to *her* like that. Or, you might contemplate the idea for a moment as you cheat on your taxes, wondering what things would be like if this whole reincarnation thing is true, and whether the $1,200 you're about to save is worth coming back as your neighbor's dog.

Indeed, the idea of reincarnation is a tough one for most to consider, let alone accept. There are, no doubt, countless reasons for why people reject the idea right away. Perhaps

Who Wants to Be a Millionaire?

A Buddhist story tells the tale of a man who gave a wandering monk food, but then, seeing it as a waste, later regretted his decision. Unbeknownst to the man, the monk was a fully enlightened being, and the karmic power of giving food to such a one was so great that the man was reborn as a millionaire for seven lifetimes. However, because he had regretted the generous act, for those seven lives he was stingy and unable to find pleasure in his riches.

due to the general rejection among modern thinkers that after death we are either sent to heaven or hell, the idea of an afterlife seems out of fashion and a hopeful artifact of the denial of death—the inability of humans to accept the end of the ego. It is the ego we are talking about, and hence a sense of self—your conscious being. When Westerners think of reincarnation, they tend to think of themselves suddenly waking up in another's body, thinking the same thoughts and feelings you did as before, except now as "Rover" you wonder why the Engletons are so stingy with those biscuits. Appears absurd and, most likely, it is.

Reincarnation = Recycling

The notion in Buddhism of reincarnation is actually quite different. Reincarnation in the Buddhist sense has more to do with the consistency of energy than the retransplanting of your exact sense of self. It parallels the scientific law of the conservation of energy—it can be neither created nor destroyed. It may be changed, but the amount of energy within a system stays the same. Karma has one property, and that is to *continue*. People die and others are born. The energy and atoms of your being simply get reabsorbed by the cosmic goo.

To take a somewhat less-than-attractive look at the issue, consider the event of your own death. If you are to be buried, you are placed under the ground, where you will slowly decompose. Maggots will feast on you and absorb the matter that constituted you. These maggots will then move on, some to be eaten by predators. In this way, the "stuff" of you continues, albeit in different shapes and forms. In essence, then, you are immortal, but your conscious, or sense of self, the "I," most likely is not. In death it is your ego that ends. Your cells and atoms, filled with your sense of purpose, strive to continue. Think of it as your atoms getting recycled and consequently redistributed.

> **KARMIC DO**
>
> Picking your fights wisely—getting a Coke when you asked for Pepsi is no cause for a conniption.
>
> **KARMIC DON'T**
>
> Flipping out because you got coleslaw instead of fries.

Take the Long-Term View

Karma guarantees the interconnectedness and interrelatedness of all things. In fact, classical Buddhist teachers maintain seeking enlightenment is meaningless if you fail to heed karma and its meaning for continuity and reincarnation. Thus it is karma that binds you to the cycle of rebirth, and the only way to transcend this and escape the cycle is to reach a state of existence in which you are no longer generating karma. Buddhists believe that grasping and attachment are the cornerstones of karma, and so the state in which you experience release is when you have become unattached and no longer grasp. By grasping at life, we continue to live under its sentence. Grasping and attachment are a result of ignorance. Since ignorance can be overcome through knowledge and learning to see the reality of things, one comes back to the Buddha's Middle Path. A misconception often made is that because of reincarnation, why try? Because we are always making new karma, and there is always the option of changing the path we're on.

Reincarnation in Hinduism: Life's a Play

The Hindu conception of reincarnation, or rebirth, is based on the existence of an *atman*, an eternal soul that continues to be reborn as it strives to reach *moksha*, the

How *Do* They Do It?

Legend tells the tale of a Buddhist monk who was challenged to prove reincarnation was real. The monk promised that he would demonstrate by dying and coming back in a way that would make it clear. He put a red mark on his forehead, a pear in his mouth, and proceeded to die. Having mastered the process, the monk was immediately reborn nearby. On the baby's head was the red mark, and in his mouth, a pearl.

Hindu equivalent of nirvana. In the play of *lila* (mentioned in the first chapter), we are all characters on the stage of life. In each lifetime we experience reincarnation through the constant reorganization of the play, different acts, and we finally decide, "Well, this approach is really not working very well," and so we take up the part of another actor whose role just became available and try it that way. Perhaps Shakespeare had found his own tree of enlightenment when he wrote, "All the world's a stage, / And all the men and women merely players." In the West, however, reincarnation has often been assumed to *be* immortality.

Reincarnation in Buddhism

In Buddhism, there are four types of rebirth. The first is to move from one life to another: You die and are then reborn. The second is intentional rebirth, such as that practiced by some Tibetan monks, or lamas, who promise to keep coming back and leading others to enlightenment. The third is spiritual rebirth, a transformation within this lifetime. Fourth, you have the moment-to-moment rebirth; that which you and I are experiencing every moment—today is a new day, and so will tomorrow be.

Unlike Hinduism, Buddhism doesn't propose the existence of an actual soul. Therefore, reincarnation in Buddhism does not involve the transfer of some thing through time and space from one body to the other. Instead, what continue are subtle levels of consciousness. Even with the lamas, who are said to be able to choose to come back over and over to continue their mission of helping others reach enlightenment, it is not believed that the child through which a lama is reincarnated is the "same" person the lama was in a past life. All that is considered to be the same is the dedication to the mission of helping others.

Lamas are born already "awake," which is exactly what the Buddha said to someone who asked him if he was a god or deity. He simply said, "I am awake." (Some believe

KARMIC DO
....
Calling to cancel your dinner reservations after you decide to eat in.

KARMIC DON'T
....
Slipping the Maitre d' a 10-spot to get you to the top of the list.

it took the Buddha himself some 500 lives to reach the lifetime in which he achieved enlightenment.)

The Chicken or the Egg?

The Dalai Lama explains the principal upon which Buddhism bases reincarnation as the "continuity of consciousness." We tend to accept the idea that if we break down the elements of the material world, we are essentially following a chain of causation that will lead us back to a point of origin for everything. In the spirit of relativity, we know the argument becomes circular as to what happened first because obviously something always preceded that which came after it: By tracing back the creation of our solar system, we arrive at stardust, which itself is the product of a previous universe that disintegrated. In this event, we've accepted that nothing suddenly springs into existence from nothing. Consciousness works the same way.

The Birth of "I"

We know we have a consciousness because we can observe it in action: We think and feel. We also know that our consciousness is inextricably connected in some way to our physical nature. It only follows, then, that there must be some method through which consciousness interacts with the physical that enables it to produce another conscious being. When two people have a baby, they don't give birth to only a physical body, they also give birth to a consciousness. So if we trace back consciousness, we are following a continuous succession of mind. While there is certainly a relationship between mind and matter, neither can be supposed to give birth to the other. From this, Buddhism deducts the pattern of rebirth. The force perpetuating the endless cycle of rebirth is karma.

The King and the Candle

The classic example given in Buddhism for reincarnation is that of the candle or oil lamp. The historical case involves a Buddhist sage and a king, and the king is asking the sage about reincarnation. He asks if, when a person dies and is reincarnated, the reincarnated person is the same person. The sage responds (as is typical in these situations) with a question. If a lamp burns all night, is the flame that burns in the first part of the night the same flame that burns at dawn? The king responds, "No." Then was there one lamp at the beginning of the night, and another lamp that burned at dawn? Again, the king responds, "No." The sage then says that this is the same as reincarnation, an ever-changing succession of something that is on the one hand the same and on the other hand different.

Rebirth in the Pool Hall and in the Garden

In the case of billiard balls, consider the momentum generated by the cue ball as karma—the driving force that impels it to move. When the cue ball hits the next ball, the cue ball changes direction, and the next ball is set in motion. The ball is different, but the momentum pushing the ball is the same. The energy has simply been transferred.

A similar parallel can be drawn between reincarnation and those perennial flowers growing in your backyard. Assuming there's no life after death, if the flowers die in the winter, technically they should not be able to return in the spring—and yet they do. So do they really die? Are they reborn? Few would argue that the flowers that arrive in the spring are the same flowers that were there the previous spring, yet they are the same "kind" of flowers and their existence is due to those that came before them. Again, it is the energy, or momentum, or karma that has continued, not the actual substance.

> **KARMIC DO**
> ....
> Taking a long, candlelit bubble bath when no one is home.
>
> **KARMIC DON'T**
> ....
> Taking a 45-minute shower first thing in the morning, using up all the hot water.

Fish Love Water—and Lots of It

WHEN SHE WAS 9 YEARS OLD, Hannah won a goldfish in a clear plastic bag at a fair for shooting enough water into the mouth of a synthetic clown to explode a balloon expanding above its head. It was the kind of gift every parent dreads having to carry around the fairgrounds for another three hours before it's time to finally go, and the kind you usually expect to last a week if it even makes it through the car ride home. Perhaps because of her mother's expressed distaste for her daughter's choice of prize ("Couldn't she have just gotten the pink teddy bear?"), the fish did survive the ride home, managed to make it through that week, and the next week, and two years later, long after the novelty of having a fish had worn off and care of Goldie had fallen to her dad, Joel, her mother would spend a few minutes each day fantasizing about ways to get rid of the fish. By the end of the second year, the fish had become an unwelcome piece of furniture to all except Joel, who had somehow managed to bond with it. Hannah's mother, Joanne, began making threats to flush it down the toilet. Joel and Hannah both protested the fate, and the fish continued.

One day when Hannah was at school, Joel was at work, and Joanne was cleaning house, the sight of the "forever fish" became too much to bear and she schemed to get rid of the fish once and for all—but would compromise and allay her guilt by skipping the toilet plan. She and her mother took the fish in the fishbowl, drove to a nearby restaurant that had a big pond along its side, and released the fish into the "wild." When Hannah and Joel learned of the release, they were somewhat bummed but took it in stride. The next day as they drove past the restaurant, something looked a bit different. Joel let out a low groan and Hannah was heard to utter, "Great, mom." The pond had been drained and perhaps, just maybe, someone's going to be coming back as a fish.

Moral of the story: Despite what we do, our underlying intentions often leak through and end up shaping the results of what we do.

CHAPTER 3

What Can You Do about Karma?

Who we are today is the result of yesterday's choices. Who we will be tomorrow is the result of today's decisions.

—Pat Messiti, motivational speaker and author

CASE STUDY
Good Karma, Good Business

MALDEN MILLS INDUSTRIES, INC., a family-owned business for several decades in Lawrence, Massachusetts, and the makers of Polartec, burned to the ground in 1995. The owner, Aaron Feuerstein, shared with his workers a deep commitment to family values and the notion of always doing the "right thing." Malden Mills employees earned 20 percent more wages than the industry average. After the fire, Feuerstein could have collected the insurance money and simply closed up shop, leaving his employees high and dry.

Instead, he made the rather unique and courageous decision to continue to support his largely immigrant workforce at full pay for three months, and promised to reemploy employees after the factory had been rebuilt, spending millions to do so. The company survived.

Six years later, in 2001, Malden Mills filed for bankruptcy. The company's attempt to stay afloat during difficult times—and Aaron Feuerstein's magnanimity and leadership—had brought the admiration and respect of American business and political leaders. Its lenders offered $20 million in funding to carry the company through its hour of need. The massive support made Malden Mills' employees some of the best-supported displaced workers in the history of Massachusetts.

Moral of the story: In some shape or form, karma always comes back to you—and such is the incentive to create and distribute good karma. In times of duress, your benevolence in the past can come back to save you.

Making Karma Work in This Lifetime

You don't get to choose how you're going to die. Or when. You can only decide how you're going to live. Now.

—Joan Baez

THE GOOD NEWS IS, we don't have to live like monks to enjoy the benefits of good karma. Life may be more complex and fast-paced now, and if the Buddha were here he might be taking just as much Prozac as the next guy and arguing with his HMO as to why he only gets three sessions a month with his therapist, but his goal would still be the same: how to navigate daily life without feeling like a doormat, wondering what he'd done to deserve the karma, why the phone company was allowed to say they'd set up his phone "between the hours of 8:00 A.M. and 5:00 P.M."

And just because some guy 2,600 years ago decided to sit under a tree for seven weeks until he "got it," should what he had to say afterward really concern us? The answer is yes.

The Same but Different

Life involves suffering, and regardless of whether you are a high-power businessperson who spends her life on the go or a regular Joe semicuriously staring at a dating service ad while riding the subway, know that everyone wrestles with the same age-old issue: how to achieve happiness. And the laws of karma always apply. As karma is nothing but the sum result of our previous actions, our lives are spent within the context of our choices. The proof of this is that we often remain our own worst enemies.

But since few of us have the time—much less the inclination—to live celibate lives or go door-to-door begging for food, the trick is to find ways to incorporate karma into our modern-day lives.

What's Dharma Got to Do with It? Bums on the Trail

Think of your dharma as driving your karma. Dharma is often loosely translated as meaning "duty." Kind of like that little voice inside that informs you, whether you listen to it or not, of what you know is right or true. In 1958, Jack Kerouac published *Dharma Bums,* which, like many of his other novels, was largely an autobiographical tale of him and his friends. In this case, among those chronicled are himself, Allen Ginsberg, Neal Cassady, and Gary Snyder. For years, Kerouac traveled the country writing books that went unpublished, and stashed each in his rucksack. Initially rejected as an author, he eventually got his first book published through the efforts of his friends. They called themselves dharma bums because they were fulfilling their spiritual duty, doing what they were meant to do. While their individual stories, as in all lives, were not filled with constant joy (and Kerouac's took a particularly sad turn to say the least, as he became disillusioned with the popular interpretation of the Beat movement, and slowly faded into obscurity), by following their "dharma" they did help to launch a cultural revolution—one that brought the idea of dharma back into popular culture. When an interviewer once told Allen Ginsberg that he considered him to be a hero of the dharma, Ginsberg replied: "I'm a dharma slob. A dharma failure." Apparently, his "humbling" trip to India worked.

> **KARMIC**
> **DO**
> ....
> Giving a surprise gift to a friend.
>
> **KARMIC**
> **DON'T**
> ....
> Receiving a gift, telling the friend how much you love it, then taking it back and exchanging it for the cash.

Being Our Own Bums

We're all on a similar mission, wondering what to do with the life that we've got, whether there's something we're supposed to be doing other than what we are, wondering

Some Things Never Change

The Greek philosopher Ptahopte, in the twenty-fourth century B.C.E., felt it necessary to exclaim, "Be happy while you are alive." A few thousand years later, Bobby McFerrin hit gold with a simple song entitled, "Don't Worry, Be Happy." People are still searching for the same thing: Happiness and feelings of contentment are just as elusive now as they were then and, regardless of how many contraptions we surround ourselves with, just like the Visa commercial, Karma is everywhere you want to be.

if we'd be playing at Carnegie Hall right now if we hadn't chosen Super Mario Brothers over the violin when we were nine, momentarily fantasizing about the idea of trying it now. In Buddhism, dharma came to be known as the teachings of the Buddha. By understanding your dharma, you can alter your karma, and by staying true to your dharma, you inevitably create good karma; it's a simple, sweet, solid relationship. To make the relationship work, we have to make a commitment to at least try to bring them closer. And fortunately, every day is a new day.

Follow Your Heart—and Your Karma

Your dharma is your essential truth; it's your will untainted by fears or cravings. When we are relaxed, feel unthreatened, and are able to look around without feeling chained to a specific emotion but can experience the range of emotions as they come and go without latching on to any one of them in particular, we are at peace, content, and in harmony. We could stay in that place for eternity. And then come the two main emotions that shape so much of our lives: fear and desire. We want this but are scared of that, we're scared of that but we want this. These emotions would dictate our lives if we let them. They are the source of our karma. When we act in accordance with our dharma we generate good karma, and when we don't, we inevitably generate bad karma, tension, and frustration. These are by definition unpleasant states, and unless we break their cycle they continue unabated. Merging our karma with our dharma is the same as forming new habits, which necessitates us breaking old ones.

The Dalai Lama has said that the way to tell the difference between a positive and a negative desire is not whether it will satisfy you right now, but whether it will result in positive or negative consequences in the long run.

Changing Karma

Maybe you never give change to someone on the street because if you can't give to everyone, why give to anyone? Certainly there are times when you walk past because you have no change, and other times you walk past with an uncomfortable bulge of coins in your pocket, get home, then complain about being stuck with all this change, which you then toss on the top of the dresser. Emptied of change the next day, you're comfortably driving around town on your day off when you blow a front tire. You head to the nearest pay phone to call AAA, and realize you're penniless.

KARMIC
DO
....

Reading a favorite book to a child.

KARMIC
DON'T
....

Turning on a video for her instead and reading your own book.

You look around, wondering if you can borrow a quarter from someone. No one has one, or, as you begin to suspect based on your own behavior, some of them probably do and they're just not giving it to you. With a soft curse, you guess, perhaps correctly, that if you were decked out in your work clothes rather than the sweats and T-shirt you're currently in, someone may have given you the quarter. What comes around goes around.

Smile as if You're Always on *Candid Camera*

If you cross a toll bridge on your way to work, smile at the attendant and enjoy the smile you get in return. If you don't get a smile, feel good that you did it anyway and that you're not responsible for spreading any bad karma. Come into work greeting everybody with a warm, "Hello," and take solace that you've done your part to spread good cheer in others.

Cleansing Bad Karma in One Swoop: Anguli Mala

Buddhism uses the legend of Anguli Mala to demonstrate that a lifetime of bad karma can still be overcome. Anguli Mala was a jungle bandit with a penchant for attacking unsuspecting travelers, on a mission to create a necklace made of 1,000 human finger bones. A rough character, indeed. On and on he went, constructing his digit necklace and becoming a total menace to the locals.

On the day when Anguli Mala had 999 bones on his necklace and could think of nothing else but getting the 1,000th, he happened to see his mother, who was coming to find him, walking through the forest. After a moment's regret over the identity of the approaching figure, he was able to gather his wits long enough to realize she'd complete his necklace, and he set out to do her in. As he neared, he noticed another person, a monk, and decided that rather than smiting his mother, he'd take the stranger instead.

Overwhelmed by the radiance of the man, who was none other than the Buddha, Anguli Mala felt his angst dissolve. He asked why this was so, and the Buddha explained that it was the result of inner peace and nirvana. Anguli Mala expressed his wish to repent, and the Buddha assured him that although he had built up enough bad karma to rival a city of thieves, karma could be changed. Anguli Mala became a devotee, and it's said that within one lifetime, Anguli Mala was able to work out his bad karma. So if finger-bone–jeweler-man could overcome the bad karma of relieving 999 people of their fingers before leaving their bodies to the crows, we should have no problem overcoming the fact that we relieved the office of two boxes of ballpoint pens and blamed it on a guest speaker once he left.

> **KARMIC**
> # DO
> ....
> Cleaning the kitchen until it sparkles as a surprise to your spouse.
>
> **KARMIC**
> # DON'T
> ....
> Leaving the gray ring in the bathtub and a hair patch in the drain.

Stay the Course

Don't let your goodwill or karma be influenced by either the positive or negative responses you get from others. Just because the toll attendant doesn't smile at you doesn't mean you shouldn't smile at him. Just because someone at work doesn't say, "Hello" when they see you first thing in the morning doesn't mean you shouldn't continue saying "Hello" to her. While at first this may seem like being a martyr every time you bump into "Hapless Bob" at 8:30 A.M. each day, eventually you will come to the realization that by continuing to greet him, you are better able to maintain your own sense of well being.

Indeed, spread the love. The more you greet people, the more likely it is that someone will give you a warm welcome and put you back in good spirits the day you come in feeling you would have been better off if you'd stayed in bed. And though tempting, just because you don't get a friendly wave when you stop at a one-lane bridge and let the person on the other side go first doesn't mean you should put a hex on their first-born. Good karma comes naturally when we accept our interdependence with others and the universe, remain nonjudgmental, accept impermanence as the natural state, and open our hearts.

The Hungry Ghost

The karma we create when we are ruled by fear and desire brings suffering and frustration into our lives. Buddhism describes the situation through the analogy of the "hungry ghost." Imagine a being with a tremendous gut, a skinny neck, and a mouth the size of the head of a pin, suffering from insatiable hunger. The hungry ghost is constantly trying to achieve the impossible: stuffing enough food through its small mouth and down its skinny neck to fill its enormous belly. It will never succeed, and incessantly attempting an impossible task creates unending suffering and frustration.

Such is the eternal headache we human folk have suffered since the beginning of time, and the reason Henry Louis Mencken saw fit to define a wealthy man as any man whose salary is $100 more a year than his "wife's sister's husband."

Desire

There are three forms of desire: the desire for sensual pleasure, the desire to exist and to continue doing so, and the desire for nonexistence. (Interesting to note that while Sigmund Freud described the "death instinct" in the early nineteenth century, the notion had already existed over 1,000 years earlier in the East.) When these desires are met with frustration, we respond with karma, and if we stubbornly continue to push for satisfaction, we're responding with negative, or unwholesome, karma, meaning we are not acting out of wisdom but out of ignorance: "And if this dead horse doesn't get up now, I swear I'll hit him again!" is still a popular, though unconscious, mantra for many of us.

We all know a lunch hour is never enough time in which to achieve anything at the DMV, and yet we'll go there anyway on our lunch break. After 45 minutes of waiting in line without even having come within spitting distance of the counter, we start seething, despite the fact that we knew this was the way it was going to go. Five minutes later when we have to go back to work empty-handed, having proven nothing except what we already knew, we can either hold on to the frustration, or simply let it go. The karma can go either way, but which way it will go is up to us.

How to Generate Good Karma

Throw your dreams into space like a kite, and you do not know what it will bring back, a new life, a new friend, a new love, or a new country.

—Anaïs Nin

SPREAD THE JOY, spread the good karma, "love the one you're with," realize things are almost never as bad as they seem. Creating good karma is amazingly rewarding: Once you start doing it, what goes around comes around, and things start falling into place as happiness begets happiness. Like pulling off the perfect béarnaise sauce, there is an art to living well. Follow your dharma; follow the Middle Path.

The Middle Path

Without question, we all have certain needs that must be met. But as the Buddha discovered over 2,500 years ago by living as both a prince and then an ascetic, neither brought him to true happiness or put an end to his suffering. The Middle Path is the route of non-extremes and of balanced living: Just because you slip after lunch and have a super double-fudge brownie when you're trying to watch your weight doesn't mean you should consider the day a defeat, throw caution to the wind because everything is ruined, and decide you might as well just eat three more.

The Middle Path is often misunderstood as meaning the path of "mediocrity"—a route that doesn't involve pushing yourself or attempting to better your current situation—but nothing could be farther from the truth. Practicing the art of living in peace while at the same time satisfying your needs is no easy task. The Middle Path is broken into eight categories specifically geared toward one of the three main components of Buddhism, each of which would make for a perfect poster in an elementary school cafeteria: Wisdom, Ethical Conduct, and Mental Discipline. All three lead to good karma.

The eight factors are right understanding, right thought, right speech, right action, right livelihood, right effort, right mindfulness, and right concentration. They are interdependent, each feeding off of and supporting the others. If there was ever a recipe for generating good karma....

> **KARMIC**
> # DO
> ....
> Listening to Shostakovich's Symphony No. 5 while quietly lying on your back.
>
> **KARMIC**
> # DON'T
> ....
> Ignoring your sleeping roommate and blasting your music when you get home at 2 A.M.

Learning from Past Mistakes

The Nepalese say: He who can't dance blames the uneven courtyard.

The West says: The unskillful carpenter blames his tools.

The Dutch say: A donkey will not stub its toe on the same stone twice.

In Bay St. Louis, Mississippi, they say: But a jackass will.

Right Thought and Right Understanding

None of us would knowingly bring pain and suffering upon ourselves, and so when we generate bad karma we do so out of ignorance. And ignorance, which forms the basis for greed, hate, and our denial of the impermanent nature of the universe, can be overcome through wisdom. At the most basic level, it's like the moment when we realize that sticking our finger into an electrical socket doesn't bring the kind of excitement we were looking for.

Right thought refers to the suppression of hate and malice in favor of love, kindness, compassion, and nonviolence. Making good karma starts here: acting with good intent. Right understanding is the ability to see clearly and understand the Four Noble Truths, which means being aware of the true sources of suffering and frustration. It is the ability to see the world without confounding distractions and therefore the ability to see things as they really are. When we are seeing things as they really are, we are no longer chained to our desires, and so we are no longer deceiving ourselves or others by behaving in ways that lead us down a road of pain and frustration, eventually causing the same in others.

Right Speech, Right Action, and Right Livelihood

Right speech, right action, and right livelihood create ethical conduct, the aim of which is to promote happiness and harmony both within and between individuals. Right speech is to use your words wisely—to not lie, slander, say things which could lead to disharmony among others, gossip or babble simply for the sake of hearing your own voice, and avoid harsh and abusive language. At this point, we're pretty much left with nothing to say except to speak the truth, use kind and benevolent language, and explain useful and constructive things to enhance feelings of unity and the spread of compassion.

> **KARMIC DO**
>
> Listening sympathetically to your friend's never-ending stories of woe.
>
> **KARMIC DON'T**
>
> Telling her to snap out of it and get a life.

Right action is to behave wisely, promoting just acts and inspiring others to do so as well. It is the physical manifestation of right thought and right speech, and it is the practicing of good karma. Acts of theft and violence will only perpetuate pain and suffering within yourself and among others. Right action is similar to the idea that you should "do unto others as you would have them do unto you." Indeed, there is little sympathy for the car thief who has his car stolen.

And speaking of car thieves, insurance scammers, ambulance chasers, telemarketers, and other folks practiced in the art of creating bad karma and spreading misery, right livelihood refers to living honorably and honestly, and through a profession that doesn't profit at the expense of others.

Right Effort, Right Mindfulness, and Right Concentration

These remaining three factors constitute mental discipline, through which the mind is trained. Right effort refers to the necessity of mental restraint, an active process of working to defuse negative and malicious thoughts in favor of positive and constructive ideas and intent. It's therefore necessary to actively work on producing positive thought processes if we are to adjust our karma for the better.

Right mindfulness is to be accurately aware of all that occurs within you—sensations of the body, emotions, and passing thoughts. It is impossible to achieve right effort if you are unaware of the times in which you are engaging in negative and destructive thoughts. Be mindful of the processes through which you construct thoughts of greed and hate and of how you can adjust your thinking to produce their opposite.

Lastly, right concentration is a description of the four stages one goes through during the process of enlightenment. In the first stage, negative and malicious thoughts, worries and doubts, and the thirst and desire for sensual pleasure give way to happiness and feelings of contentment. In the second stage, faculties of the intellect and constant analysis dissolve, while the sense of joy and contentment remain. In the third stage, joy, which is a desire and reflects thirst, disappears, leaving only the feeling of contentedness and the additional awareness of equanimity. In the final stage, all sensations, happy and sad, give way to a sense of unity, and all that is left is the awareness of being and of pure equanimity. It almost seems to mirror the act of falling asleep, as your active mind slowly shuts down, your worries dissolve, and hopes and any delusions of grandeur gently subside into the calm stillness of rest.

> **KARMIC**
> ## DO
> ....
> Washing and vacuuming your parents' car after they loan it to you.
>
> **KARMIC**
> ## DON'T
> ....
> Bringing the car back on Empty.

Living in the Here and Now

Despite our efforts to do so, it can be difficult to fully experience your life in the here and now. It's especially difficult when so much of your life is spent living under the perspective of linear time as representing reality. In linear time cause and effect are separated by time and space, and so the past seems like the only stable and concrete time period we can talk or think about. The present moment, or the now, seems almost insignificant because,

Being Present in the Present

When we get mentally lost in a time other than now, we have, so to speak, "left the building." The emotional weight of worries, regrets, dashed hopes, and anxious thoughts of the future can feel like a physical weight, and it becomes difficult to maintain a sense of perspective and fend off tunnel vision. Next time you're there, try these steps:

1) Take a moment and become aware of what thoughts and feelings you're having.

2) Recognize that the feelings and thoughts are actually weightless, transitory, and fleeting; but you must allow them to be that.

3) Let them go.

4) Look out a window, and take three slow, deep breaths, being aware of how each feels from the intake into your chest through your nose; while you exhale, remain aware of the same things.

according to our clocks, now lasts for only an instant: The moment we think of it, time has already moved forth and the now has already become the past. The future exists only as an abstraction, for we can do little other than guess at what it may hold in store.

It becomes almost too easy to spend all of our time in the now thinking about things that are either gone or things that haven't happened yet—with the result that we live much of the now on autopilot, unaware of the karmic power we have in each moment and unaware of the effects we are currently creating.

Meet Your Gestalt

Despite rumblings about rebirth and the idea that we might come back a gazillion times before we get the hang of things, the practical approach to mastering our own karma begins with the life we're in—after all, we're here now, the plumber is coming at 3:00 P.M. to unclog the sink, and most likely, he'd rather have our cash than the promise of good karma when all is said and done. Indeed, most of us have a hard enough time trying to successfully plan for next week, let alone coordinating our next move to get a good seat in the next life. So how do we bring notions of karma and reincarnation to bear on the right here, right now? It's actually not that big a leap.

Just Do It

Chad Pregracke, a 25-year-old, has been personally cleaning up the Mississippi River for a period of four years. He's cleaned up 1,500 miles of shoreline and collected 400,000 pounds of trash. He says, "I just got tired of seeing all the garbage lying around. I didn't want to talk about it, I just wanted to get it done. So I did it myself."

Rebecca Yenawine, a 27-year-old visual artist who bought a house in a dilapidated section of Baltimore, noticed a number of teenage girls spray-painting graffiti in the area, so she brought them home and gave them an art lesson. Ever since, she's held free classes for inner-city kids and started a nonprofit organization, "Kids on the Hill." Since starting, Rebecca has taken more than 100 kids off the streets and placed them into constructive after-school activities.

Frank Gantz, a 78-year-old, has since his retirement spent time clearing land and forging hiking trails for the public. Frank has created nearly 50 miles of trails to the absolute delight of thousands of hikers.

Elliot Fiks, a restaurateur who noticed all the food that was being thrown away in the process of cooking, began saving the leftovers. He started making soups to give to local soup kitchens. Over the four years he's been doing this, he's produced over 17,000 meals for those in need.

Karma describes the interdependence and unity of all events and things in the universe. Think of the universe as a kiddie pool and our karma like small stones falling into the pool. Each "plop" causes a disturbance, ripples are sent out, and these waves then converge with each other in countless directions and places and eventually return back to the same point from which they started. Looking at the activity of the pool, there's no way to determine what was causing what to happen, or which ripple started first. So instead of a clear succession of one event causing another, we have the impression of a constantly rearranging "now."

> ### KARMIC
> # DO
> ....
> **Planting a garden with lots of bulbs that come up in March to ring in spring.**
>
> ### KARMIC
> # DON'T
> ....
> **Quickly snipping your neighbor's flowers to bring a bouquet to a friend's housewarming.**

Each moment, each "now," is like a *gestalt,* a term in psychology describing, in the words of Merriam-Webster, "a structure, configuration, or pattern of physical, biological, or psychological phenomena so integrated as to constitute a functional unit with properties not derivable by summation of its parts." The now is like an endlessly rearranging and reconverging gestalt of what just "was" merged with what is "now."

The main controlling and defining factor in what is now is karma, which guides the rearranging gestalt. The cause of the current gestalt is impossible to determine precisely because it is a result of *everything* which just was and now *is*. With this perspective, the most important time to be concerned with is now. Every moment is a new now, and in each moment we are given the opportunity to change our karma and therefore the course of what will happen next.

The Courage to Change

We can always change, but we tend to fear unchartered territory. To laugh at oneself after a lifetime of not being able to is a scary prospect until we try it. To go out dancing when we've spent years insisting we can't dance creates anxiety, at which point we are liable to lie to friends as to the reason we can't go out, maintaining we have other plans. We are then faced with either having to maintain the lie or looking silly when they later call and find us still at home. Deception breeds deception and creates self-loathing, and if we are unaware of this we may fall into the trap of trying to transfer the negative feelings to someone else so we feel free of it. When we do this, we continue the spread of negative karma.

Get Me Outta Here—
How to Avoid Bad Karma

*If you realized how powerful your thoughts are,
you would never think a negative thought...*

—Peace Pilgrim, activist

HOW BAD IS BAD? By understanding what bad karma is and how it functions, we're that much closer to discovering how to transform it into positive karma. Bad karma, or *akshula,* refers to an unwise course of action that inevitably results in suffering and frustration for oneself and others. It was an "unwise" decision that led my friend in sixth grade to holler, "Hey! Buffalo Butt!" at an eighth-grader three times his size. As a result, he quickly became the only kid I knew who could describe, from first-hand experience, what it feels like to have your head rammed into the side of school bus.

This Bad...

Bad karma comes out in three ways: through our body, speech, and mind. Buddhism proposes that there are three unwholesome, or negative, actions of the body, four of speech, and three of mind. Any act based on one of these is destined to result in bad karma. The actions of the body seen as unwholesome are theft, disrespectful use of sexuality, and physical violence. The four means through which bad karma is propagated by speech are malicious gossip, slander, abusive language, and deceit. For the mind, the three negative acts are anger, delusion, and greed. For negative karma to achieve full force, an act must: 1) have been done intentionally; 2) been completed; 3) have been committed without remorse; and 4) been done without a promise to never repeat the act again.

Askin' for Trouble

If we understand karma as similar to laws of attraction and the idea that "like begets like," it becomes clear that practicing bad karma is akin to running around on a golf course with a twelve-iron during a lightning storm. When we're angry, we attract anger. When we're depressed, we attract more depression. Misery loves company. We can become like self-fulfilling prophecies. People seething with frustration and looking for an outlet go looking for fights and generally find them. An alcoholic who says marital discord causes him to drink will often begin an argument to legitimize having to go out to the bars and let off some steam. People looking for help will do things to attract it. A jealous heart becomes more jealous.

What goes around comes around: If we throw a boomerang we shouldn't expect it to come back in the shape of a Frisbee. And so one of the greatest things we can do to avoid bad karma is to become aware of our thoughts, the behavior they lead to, and the results or effects they produce.

Constant Craving = Constant Meddling

We like to feel in control, so we incessantly meddle with things, trying our best to shape the outcome of events to our liking. If controlled the slot machine we would win every time; if we controlled the courts we would never get a ticket; if we controlled the weather it would always be "perfect;" if we controlled people we would always get what we wanted; if we controlled the economy we would get everything for free. Alas, we actually control very little, but that doesn't keep us from trying. By our very nature, we are *meddlers,* and for the most part, when we meddle with things we tend to mess them up. And when we meddle with karma, karma meddles with us, and in the end the joke's on us.

> **KARMIC
> DO**
> ....
> Giving a loving hug
> to your sibling.
>
> **KARMIC
> DON'T**
> ....
> Refusing to loan him
> your favorite CD.

Let Go

There's a saying in Buddhism: "That which you most desire will be your biggest problem." If we are unable to take ourselves lightly and give a good chuckle at our faults, we invite humiliation, for no one is perfect. We say stupid things when we are trying our hardest not to say them, we look the silliest when we are attempting look our most serious, we become angry when we are trying our hardest to be happy, we fall when we are trying our hardest not to lose our balance, and we explode with laughter in moments when we are trying our hardest to be stern.

We must learn to let go and let things come as they may. Herman Hesse set it straight when he said, "Some of us think holding on makes us strong; but sometimes it is letting go." We need to practice letting things play out rather than trying to control them from the very outset. Karma is a potent force, and we benefit only when we're careful about where we toss it.

Three Wishes, and None Turned Out Right

The granting of wishes is something every kid dreams of and the thing that most adults have learned isn't always all it's cracked up to be—for sometimes we actually do get what we wish for, and it isn't at all what we expected.

The Truth about Change

A mother dies and leaves two rings: one diamond and the other silver. Enthralled by the diamond ring, the elder sister quickly chooses it. While the younger sister understood why her mother kept the diamond ring, she didn't see much value in the silver one. When she looked at the ring more carefully, however, she saw the words, "This will also change," etched into it. The older sister went on to live life tense, anxious, and chained to her emotions. But the younger sister rode the flow of change, never becoming attached to any one moment. In tough times, she'd simply look at her ring, remembering, "This will also change."

King Midas was none too pleased when he got what he'd wished for—and therein lies the tricky part about karma, which is exactly what the Buddha spent the second half of his life explaining: Our desires are the root cause of our suffering. That expensive foreign car will be just as expensive to fix, that house advertised as a "fixer-upper" will most likely require just that, and the puppy we wanted because it was going to be so cute and fuzzy will also need to go for walks in the winter, chew through our CD collection, and put a few landmines in the living room before all is said and done.

When these things happen, we tend to look at them as mistakes, accidents, something that went wrong, or something that shouldn't have happened. But these are the realities of life. Alan Watts once commented that the reason genies always give three wishes is so that after the first two totally backfire, we can use the third to get back to where we were before we rubbed the lamp.

Never Say Forever

Buddhism is a philosophy that holds impermanence as an essential aspect of both ourselves and the universe. Feelings, thoughts, and objects themselves are fleeting and subject to change; nothing is forever. Depression offers a good parallel to the issue. Depression affects our perceptions and is analogous to the Buddhist view that suffering begins in the mind. When we are depressed, our perception of time is that it slows down, and since we gauge change by time, change also slows down, almost to a standstill.

The impression then is that the way we feel now and that the way things are will never change, and what we are experiencing now will last for eternity. As opposed to the general attitude in the West of always looking toward the future and forgetting that we exist solely in the now, the

KARMIC
DO
Making an apple pie and bringing it to a neighbor who lives alone.

KARMIC
DON'T
Stealing some apples from your neighbor's tree while he's on vacation and then blaming it on the neighborhood kids.

depressive mind becomes eternally trapped in the now, seeing no end to it; "I will always feel this way," becomes the mantra, and we are essentially trapped in the Buddha's first noble truth, that life is suffering, and forget that it can be overcome.

A butterfly in Japan just flapped its wings, and the weather over Idaho is about to change because of it. You were plodding through another routine day at the office thinking about the boring evening ahead and wondering, "Is this all that life has to offer me?" when a friend suddenly calls and invites you to a concert later that evening. Now you're ecstatic, you feel differently, life is good, the feeling is somewhat infectious to your coworkers as you become more energized, you call up somebody else to see if they want to go as well—everything is different now.

I remember going through a difficult time in my life, having breakfast at a diner and looking like a wreck, and the waitress leaned toward me as she refilled my coffee and said, "This, too, shall pass." True wisdom delivered over black coffee and hastily prepared French toast. As John Lennon sang, "Instant karma's gonna get you."

Change Is Good

When we fight change, we generate bad karma in our attempts to control the uncontrollable. Imagine buying an expensive set of china. It's fragile, and every time you or someone else in your family touches it your heart gives a brief skip as you pray, "Don't drop it!" You want to use it at dinner parties, yet it makes you anxious at the same time. You enter into emotional conflict and end up realizing you'd have a better time if everyone would just use paper plates and plastic forks and not think anything of it. When we take the approach that "the glass is already broken," life is simpler and more pleasant. It is learning to let go.

If, however, you accept the union of opposites and see change and decay as two sides of the same coin, neither better than the other, things start to appear differently. When you look at the intact china, you can also see and be aware of the potential cracks. On the inevitable day that a piece breaks, you are not destroyed because you already knew that this was a natural consequence of owning it in the first place. Like life, you enjoyed it while you had it. It is not the guy who dies with the most toys in the attic who wins, but the person who enjoyed the ones he had while he was alive—regardless of how many of them broke along the way.

When Bad Things Happen to Good People

> *You don't need a weatherman to know which way the wind blows.*
>
> —Bob Dylan, "Subterranean Homesick Blues"

LIFE HAPPENS, $#%@ happens, what happens *happens*, but it is never *fate*. Fate suggests that "things happen for a reason," that there is an ultimate moral goal or script that the universe follows. But things don't happen for a reason other than the reason that things just happen. You're walking with a group of friends and then it happens: Either you had a target on the top of your head or the wind was just blowing in the right direction, but you feel a quick "spat!" on your head and look up just in time to see the offending bird. And you're left thinking, "What did I do to deserve that?" Quite possibly, nothing; things happen to people, it is a natural result of being alive. If nothing ever happens to you, something is terribly amiss.

Hey! What's the Deal? I Didn't Deserve That!

And yet the question of karma begs the issue: If we are

the sum of all of our previous actions and like action begets like results, how do you explain "when bad things happen to good people?" I was a good guy all this week, and then I got shafted at work. That wasn't fair; did I do something bad? Did everyone who went down on the *Titanic* deserve it? Did any of us deserve the Teletubbies? Did someone conduct a survey in which respondents overwhelmingly thought infomercials would be a great idea and that insomniacs would like to have some more options?

The karma of individuals interacts with collective karma, which interacts with the karma of the cosmos.

> **KARMIC**
> **DO**
> ·······················
> Picking up a stray kitten and finding it a home.
>
> **KARMIC**
> **DON'T**
> ·······················
> Hurling slurs at your pet because you've had a bad day.

Thus, some will suffer, seemingly undeservedly, because of the actions of humanity and because no matter how "good" any one person is, he or she cannot live life fully insulated from the actions of others or from those of the universe at large. And so we find our rakes occasionally stolen, our sandcastles smashed by mischievous feet, the crossword puzzle missing from the Sunday *New York Times Magazine*.

Humans can be harsh and unforgiving, humans live in a world that can be harsh and unforgiving, and so humans

Unmerited Suffering

"Personal trials have taught me the value of unmerited suffering. As my suffering mounted I soon realized that there were two ways in which I could respond to my situation...react with bitterness or seek to transform the suffering. I decided to follow the latter course. Recognizing the necessity for suffering, I have tried to make of it a virtue. If only to save myself from bitterness, I have attempted to see my personal ordeals as an opportunity to transfigure myself and heal the people involved in the tragic situation which now obtains. I have lived these last few years with the conviction that unearned suffering is redemptive."

—Martin Luther King Jr.

will inevitably at times experience just that. Suffering, like karma, is a universal fact. Everyone has felt pain, certainly some more than others, but as yet, there has not been a single being alive that has lived in a constant state of bliss from beginning to end.

Karma Stops for No One

And yet the law of karma is neutral, morality completely absent. Whether a good man or a bad man should fall off a cliff, gravity will treat him no differently. What we have a difficult time understanding is that we always want to know the cause of our pain, or of what we believe to be "good" or "bad" so that we can control it. We have, however, control over nothing but ourselves, and therefore the only thing we have control over is our response to our environment. No one *makes* us feel a certain way, though we are often quick to say, "That made me angry." It may well be justified, but we are still responsible for our reaction; the other person is not.

The idea of unmerited suffering can strike us as hopelessly unjust, and yet suffering is an inherent aspect of being alive. Karma is not supernatural, and thus miracles should not be supposed. Since the ultimate goal is to achieve universal harmony, the law of karma must apply evenly and consistently on both the micro and macro levels. We create the karma of suffering for ourselves and for others through our attachment and clinging to the notion of "I." The notion of "I" is a manifestation of our basic will and desire to exist and to experience pleasure. In short, it really is "ego."

> **KARMIC DO**
> ·················
> Singing softly to rock a baby to sleep.
>
> **KARMIC DON'T**
> ·················
> Letting her cry herself to sleep.

"Not It," with Fingertip on the Nose

By believing in the reality of an "I," we suffer the delusion that we are in fact separate from everybody else and so become fully absorbed by our own needs. We end up running the world, with a population of almost 6 billion people, under the doctrine of "every man for himself." While many of us might wish things were different, we tend to continue on this course because this is the way everyone else is acting, and "Why should I be the martyr?" We assume that since everyone else is out for himself, no is looking out for us, so that is a job left to us. We then turn away from helping others with arguments like, "Since I can't change the world, why should I try?" or, "I can't make a difference." In a society that has largely ruled out the ideas of fate and destiny, we continue to live under a rather fatalist doctrine.

How to Make Sure Your Enemies Get Their Due

Always forgive your enemies; nothing annoys them so much.

—Oscar Wilde

"AN EYE FOR AN EYE, a tooth for a tooth," sounds delicious and just. Still, as Gandhi once said and innumerable bumper stickers remind us, an eye for an eye will eventually make the whole world blind. But there is no denying that an aspect of human nature always tempts us with the idea that when we feel wronged, a little retribution will make us feel a whole lot better. We've all watched movies in which we can't wait for the bad guy to "get it." We want payback—"I hope he rots in hell"—because the whole idea of turning the other cheek leaves a bad taste in the mouth, and martyrdom seems unattractive.

> ## KARMIC DO
>
> Staying late to finish up some work for your boss who's really stressed.
>
> ## KARMIC DON'T
>
> Calling in sick after you stayed up all night partying.

The truth, however, is that acts of retribution only come back at us, for all acts are karmic, and our karma always comes back around. If someone has caused us harm, they will suffer their own karmic fruit, whether it be through guilt or simply the negative results of poor choices and behavior; it is completely impossible for anyone to escape the consequences of their actions. Again, this is not something to be taken on faith, but something to be observed.

I can remember watching a neighbor leave her house in the morning and seeing with disgust that her car had been boxed in by the cars in front and back. After looking around to see if she could locate at least one of the perpetrators, she clenched her teeth and got into her car with an air of indignation. I then watched her repeatedly shift from first to reverse, cosmetically changing the shape of the bumpers on both the car in front and the car in back of her, her facial expression one of both glee and anger. Whatever pleasure she experienced initially wore off when she got out of her car and noticed she had rearranged her front grill and rear bumper as well. A victim of her own retribution.

Resolve without Aggression

Obviously, there are different types of enemies, and it's important to remember that there is both good and bad karma, and that in many situations non-action equals bad karma. Suffice it to say, Martin Luther King could have uttered nothing closer to the truth when he proclaimed while accepting his Nobel Peace Prize that nonviolence was the answer to political issues, and that it was crucial people learn to overcome oppression and violence without committing oppression and violence themselves. He believed people needed to develop a method that could resolve conflicts without "revenge, aggression, and retaliation," and that the basis of that method would be none other than love. Amen to that.

But what we are talking about here is the following: We all have people we would put a hex on if we only knew how—a boss, a coworker, a celebrity that annoys us to no end, our sister-in-law who insists on always bringing her hyper terrier when she comes to dinner, the guy in perfect shape who feels entitled to park in the handicapped space, the people who decide to balance their checkbooks while at the drive-through ATM.

Case of the Speeding Grapefruit

A friend of mine once blew through a crosswalk in an enormous Dodge pickup, coming dangerously close to a guy trying to make it across the street but who was also ignoring the flashing "Don't Walk" sign. With a scream, the guy pulled a grapefruit out of his shopping bag, launched it at my friend's truck, and splattered it against the rear window of the cab.

How do we interpret this situation? Each brought it upon himself. The pedestrian felt entitled to just stroll through an intersection, my friend felt he could just blow past him. The pedestrian received a scare, my friend a grapefruit. Social dynamics at their best. If each person left the scene aware of his behavior and the consequences it brought,

> **KARMIC DO**
> ....
> Writing a personal note to someone who's grieving.
>
> **KARMIC DON'T**
> ....
> Sending a printed card with your name scribbled at the bottom.

they each might have had a quick chuckle at the sequence of events and continued on with the day.

Perpetuating What's Already Over and Done With

But if each becomes indignant and leaves the scene blaming the other person in entirety, the negative emotions will be perpetuated throughout the day: "Well, maybe I shouldn't have just walked out like that, but THAT guy was a total idiot flying through…" or "Well, maybe I shouldn't have just been flying through like that, but THAT nuthead walked out like…" Each may still be stewing hours after the whole thing actually happened, continuing to keep the initial feelings alive, giving them more validation, becoming more and more attached to the anger.

Perpetuating the spread of bad karma, they may continue in foul moods throughout the day, throwing dark shadows on everyone they meet. But given a moment of thought, there was really no reason to keep the ordeal alive since the situation had already ended with a solution that resulted in balance: a scare and a grapefruit. Why make it more?

Right Back at Us

Our anger has a way of bouncing back at us with the same force with which we sent it out. I remember walking through a parking lot as a kid with a friend during the winter. Full of pent-up aimlessness, I was searching for a release. I noticed a chunk of ice frozen to the pavement and, deciding that it deserved to absorb my frustration, I wound up and gave it a kick to send it across the lot. Apparently its hold on the ground was stronger than my kick, for it didn't move an inch. There I went, landing a good face-plant on the drugstore parking lot—to the absolute delight of my friend and a few passersby.

During the same time period there was a kid who lived on my block who ended up being the butt of a joke by a bunch of other kids while playing a game of touch football. An hour or so later, having had time to work out his revenge, he went down to the house where one of his tormentors lived, intending to slug him the moment he opened the door. He rang the doorbell, the door opened, he swung, he missed, and he had only a moment to regret his plan before his fist slammed into the stucco exterior of the house.

In any event, when we desire or cause some social damage or physical calamity to someone in order to make ourselves feel better, we will eventually bear the karmic fruit of the actions, be it now or later. Through either guilt, shame, or public humiliation at a cocktail party where you recently degenerated to your five-year-old self and lashed out at your neighbor, it all comes back. In addition, true poetic justice occurs only when our enemies fall prey to their own karma.

Don't Be Too Quick to Judge

A CHINESE PARABLE tells the tale of a peasant who had a son whom he cherished and a white stallion that was his most prized possession. One day, the stallion broke free and ran away. The villagers came to the man to offer their sympathies, saying that he was such an unlucky man, and that the situation was a sorry state of affairs. The peasant answered, "Who knows. Maybe it's good, maybe it's bad." The next day, his horse reappeared, with a dozen wild horses in tow. Once again, the villagers came to his home, but this time they envied him, telling him what a lucky a man he was. And again, he replied, "Who knows. Maybe it's good, maybe it's bad."

A day later his son was trying to break one of the wild horses when he fell and broke his leg. When the villagers came to the father to express their condolences over the sad state of affairs and to offer their sympathies to the man who, in their eyes, was truly an unlucky man, he replied, "Who knows.

KARMIC DO

Reading the newspaper, watching the news, knowing what's happening in the world.

KARMIC DON'T

Reading just the comics and your horoscope. (The world will take care of itself.)

Maybe it's good, maybe it's bad."

While his son was limping around the village, the emperor's army came through several days later and conscripted all the young men. Upon seeing the young man with the bad leg, they left him as unfit. The villagers couldn't believe his luck and exclaimed that surely he and his father were truly blessed men. And once again, the father replied with, "Who knows. Maybe it's good, maybe it's bad."

Moral of the story: Don't be so quick to judge your situation as good or bad—what may at first appear to be a curse often turns out later to be a blessing in disguise.

CHAPTER 4

Karmic Relationships

Love is a fire. But whether it is going to warm your heart or burn down your house, you can never tell.

—Joan Crawford

CASE STUDY
"Couldn't You Have Told Me...?"

LEE, A WRITER AND RADIO COMMENTATOR, was married for 15 years and had a 10-year-old daughter when her husband left her for a beautiful young woman. She moved out, and her husband and his new girlfriend lived together in the house that Lee and her husband had once shared, making love in the same bed and cooking on the same stove. After a couple of years of living in this situation, the house they shared burned down. Lee secretly blamed herself, thinking that if a person had focused "so much hate" on a location, the emotions would generate their own hate. Meanwhile, distraught and feeling sentimental, her husband drove all over town, mostly revisiting places that he and his ex-wife had lived together. On his way back to his girlfriend, he crashed his car.

Soon after the fire, his girlfriend realized she was a lesbian, explained to him that she now understood she'd been one for years, and dumped him. His daughter was a bit devastated herself, having grown to really love his girlfriend, and yet she was impressed by the woman's honesty, giving her the courage herself to come out as a lesbian. Over the years, both the mother and daughter have become close to the ex-girlfriend, the mother realizing she should never have felt such hostility toward her in the first place. The husband, devastated, feels now as if he's lost his wife, his home, his daughter, his car, and his girlfriend.

Moral of the story: Often, thinking that the grass is greener on the other side, we make rash decisions, only to regret them later when we discover that we weren't thinking clearly at the time we made them.

Love—If You Want It, Come and Get It

Love: The irresistible desire to be irresistibly desired.

—Mark Twain

FEELINGS OF LOVE can make or break us, and this is as true now as it was in the first century B.C.E. when Virgil exclaimed, "Love conquers all things; let us too surrender to Love." Few things can turn a renowned stoic beet red quicker than a flirtatious comment from an attractive person. Though we may pride ourselves on being reasonable people with but a few superstitions, when it comes to issues of love and sex, even the most reserved among us have gone rustling through the newspaper for our horoscope.

Love makes us feel wanted, cherished, and part of something larger than ourselves; it makes us feel whole. Love can give us a sense of purpose, bring out the best in us, and tug on our heartstrings in a way that can make us feel either invincible or like a turtle caught without a shell. Love goes straight to our core and will throw even the best of us for a loop.

Running Out of Daisies

One needn't go far to see just how deep issues of love go and the extent to which we'll go to find it. Search the Internet for "karmic love," and you'll find an endless number of glorified 1-900-number Web sites promising to read your astrological charts and get back to you with the perfect "love mixture" based on the stars and your karma, "all for only $19.95." And who would pass up—for a mere 20 bucks—the chance to meet an anonymous person over the Internet that a database has most likely chosen at random to be your "Twin Flame?" Or your "Karmic Soul Mate?" Your "Task Companion?"

There is no shortage of folks who will analyze the karmic qualities of your relationship. They might tell you that you knew the person you're currently with in a past life and that you're still working out your karma together. Or tell you that only two out of ten relationships have anything to do with love, for the other eight are just karmic mishaps. And, of course, the reason your boyfriend is making eyes at your best friend is because he was a cockroach in a past life—and you can find solace in the fact that he'll probably be one again in the next life.

Horoscope or Horrorscope?

The problem with giving too much credit to any of the above is the association of karma with fate or destiny. Consulting the stars for karmic relationships suggests there is something that is "meant to be"—rather than placing emphasis on how you deal with what you have. If you're in love and your birth chart suggests you and your lover won't last, should you run home and end the relationship now because it's doomed? Hopefully, you wouldn't. You are in control of your own karma.

The Karmic Path to Love

Put your hand on a hot stove for a minute, and it seems like an hour. Sit with a pretty girl for an hour, and it seems like a minute. THAT'S relativity.

—Albert Einstein

TRUE LOVE BEGINS with a love of the intrinsic beauty within ourselves. By loving that which is in you, you inevitably end up loving those around you. It's not naive, and you are not just opening yourself up for trouble. This is a perspective based on true strength and security, for it takes confidence to expose yourself in this way.

> ### KARMIC
> ## DO
> ....
> **Sitting quietly by a pond and reading a book of poems.**
>
> ### KARMIC
> ## DON'T
> ....
> **Throwing pebbles at the ducks to see them fly.**

All relationships are tricky, but learning to navigate them with grace can be a beautiful thing, and in feeling beautiful, loved, and giving love, our intent and motives become pure and healthy because we are no longer trying to pass off our negative emotions on others. When we are filled with concern for others we are adding to the bin of good collective karma. When we are friendlier with strangers, feel at one with nature and thereby connected to things, we lose the desire and need to exert control and manipulate. We have reached a state in which we have freed ourselves of negative karma.

I Love You Anyway

True love is when you couldn't care less if your partner likes to put anchovies on his toast and peanut butter. You want to stay home and make her tea and soup when she's not feeling well. You spontaneously want to call him just to see what's going on. True love is not possessive but all-encompassing and includes loving the life your "other half" has that is independent of you. You love your partner when she or he is mad, sad, happy, funny, weird, semi-embarrassing, dorky, annoying, dreamy, boring, exciting, reserved, flamboyant, and the biggest thorn in your side. We love our partners for their essence. When we have this kind of love, we cease creating negative karma within the relationship, for we want nothing more than for them to simply be themselves. We have stopped meddling.

The Karmic Path to Love

Love is an organic process, and we can't enjoy only the parts of it we like. With love comes the potential for hurt, and when we open ourselves, we open ourselves to potential rejection. But the simple fact is, you can't steal second until you let go of first—and experiencing love is pretty similar.

Love yourself: Because you gotta start somewhere, this is the place to start. If you don't love yourself, there's little you can do for anybody else. The wish to be loved begins with yourself; after that, you are no longer desperate and are simply looking for someone *you* can love and that will make you feel good as well. True love is when you've become able to express your love for all beings, not just those who give it back to you.

KARMIC DO

....

Voting.

KARMIC DON'T

....

Not voting. (What difference can one person make, anyway?)

Open yourself: True love is possible only when you let down your guard and risk showing your belly. Trying to give somebody a hug with your arms crossed in front of your chest is more like playing bumper cars than a game of Twister. When you've embraced yourself, others can feel the positive karma and will feel naturally drawn to you. Embrace others, give lots of hugs, and experience good karma.

Don't get it all from one place: Attempting to get all your needs met by one person not only is impossible but also will most likely send him packing or running for cover. Nobody wants to be with a person whose intent is to absorb all of her energy, 24/7. Get a life, then a relationship.

Understand the difference between love and sex: Sex by itself is not love. Having sex with someone you love is. Sex by itself is an expression of desire, like wanting to eat a piece of cake. It may be delicious, but once it's over, it's gone. Real love is a constant. Confusing sex for love is like picking a flower rather than planting one.

Find a union that works: Trying to maintain a relationship with a person who would rather not have one is like trying to sell renter's insurance to someone who owns their own home. Ask yourself what you're looking for in a relationship, then find someone who fits the bill rather than finding someone and then trying to extract from them what you're looking for in a relationship. Trying to buy a Volkswagen bug at the Chevy dealer is bound to end in frustration.

Let go of the ego: True love is an appreciation of the experience of unity. If you remain chained to your ego as being an independent and separate entity in isolation from everything else, you can't spiritually join in a relationship with anybody. A relationship based on "everyone for himself" will go nowhere.

Put those squabbles in perspective: They're inevitable. But if you've discovered a love for yourself and thus for others, if you remain open to change, if you're in love with the person you're with and not just with them for convenient sex, if you're in a relationship based on a union of equality, and if you're not so tied to your ego that you feel threatened if you're shown to be wrong, you can actually have a pretty good time when disagreements arise. Have fun. Observe with humor that you've become so emotional you're not even thinking straight and have become as stubborn as a five-year-old. Look at your partner doing the same. Now you're having fun.

If You Love Someone, Set Her Free

Love, like happiness, can become elusive when we don't actually know what it looks like. Difficulties come about through equating the extent to which we desire something as a sign of love. "I love mocha chip ice cream" has more to do with my own enjoyment of its taste and preference for it over marshmallow-fudge-swirl than an expression of a deep reciprocal relationship that exists between the ice cream and me. If I take a bite and menacingly growl, "I love *my* mocha chip ice cream," I suggest that not only do I really like it but I might seriously hurt the person who dares to try and take it from me.

When love is expressed more as a warning to others to stay away from what is yours, things can get ugly, for this is not love but desire and craving. When we strive for something based only on desire, we wish to consume it, make it a part of ourselves. This kind of love is smothering and is actually aggressive. We are turning love into an obsession for something that we greedily and possessively protect. In doing so we destroy the object of our love.

I Like It When You...

Karma describes the extraordinary as well as the completely mundane aspects of everyday life. When you drop your toothbrush on the floor of the bathroom and the next day you find it back in the holder because you were nice to your kid in the morning and she felt like doing something nice for you, that is karma. When you drop your toothbrush on the floor of the bathroom and the next day it's still on the floor in the bathroom because you were in a foul mood and no one really felt you deserved the pleasure of finding your toothbrush back in the holder, that is also karma.

> **KARMIC**
> # DO
> ....
> Turning on your sprinklers on a hot day and inviting the neighborhood kids over.
>
> **KARMIC**
> # DON'T
> ....
> Shutting the blinds, turning on the AC, and hoping it's cooler tomorrow.

It is the true lesson of karma that you get what you give. If you want to be treated as an equal in a relationship, you must treat the other person as an equal. Behaving any other way creates an imbalance, and in an attempt to restore balance to the relationship, friction is inevitable. If you wish your partner would bring you a cup of coffee in the morning when he goes into the kitchen to get his, start doing it for him. If you wish your partner would give you a hug when you walk in the door, be the first to give her one. If you wish your partner didn't put the toothpaste cap directly on the sink with the result that there are 14 blue rings on the basin by the end of the week…buy a pump.

KARMIC DO

Taking a potted plant to a friend.

KARMIC DON'T

Giving a plastic daisy. (It'll last longer.)

Love to Stay Away From

*Do you love me because I am beautiful, or am
I beautiful because you love me?*

—Cinderella

POSSESSIVE LOVE stems from insecurity and greed.
There is a wish to swallow, to consume, and to own the
person or thing. The strength or intensity of desire is a
reflection of what we think we are currently lacking. This
is not love, but an expression of our desperation to feel
whole. Attempting to take something and make it ours is
aggressive and violent, for it is about subjugating another
soul to boost one's own ego. It's unhealthy, it's bad karma,
and it will only bring about suffering. Those who try to
put a leash on another's freedom are not free themselves.
Most of us know people who have been in such relationships, have perhaps been in them ourselves, and can see
that these are not unions but a chain gang of two.

Looking for Love in All the Wrong Places

If we have lost touch with both ourself and the true
nature of the world around us we feel empty, and we will
constantly be searching for something to make us feel

whole. If it's love, then love becomes a commodity, a scarce resource, something that we try all sorts of different ways to get. Often we have shoved true love so deep down inside ourselves that we can no longer even recognize it. Love then becomes something that we lack, and therefore something that only someone or something else can give us. If we are not in possession of it, it then seems to make sense that we also don't have any to give. If love is a commodity and we finally think we've found "some," there is an instinct to be careful of how much we give and to whom—because we might give it all away. Too many of us end up protecting the amount we believe we have, guarding it with the same intensity Golem showed his ring.

Love is the double-edged sword that can heal as well as it cuts. If we are under the illusion that love is an external commodity available for consumption, we may fantasize that perhaps someday, someone will manage to package it into a free small plastic gizmo we can find at the bottom of a cereal box. The more we are obsessed and dominated by our wants and terrors, the more we become imprisoned within ourselves, cut off from others and life by an artificial boundary. It is the result of self-obsession. When we are self-obsessed, we limit our capacity and ability to interact naturally with others.

The White Elephant

As with almost anything, the harder we look for love the harder it can be to find, and herein lies the paradox: We tend to find love with a partner when we are least looking for it. Often, it seems that just when we were about to finally resign ourselves to living in a nunnery or comforting ourselves with the infamous, "Well, at least I have my career…" a person will suddenly waltz into our lives.

A man once went to the Buddha and asked how he could achieve enlightenment. He was desperate to do so, and wanted the Buddha to give him the answer. The Buddha told him to go out for a week and think of anything except for a white elephant. "Easy enough," the man thought to himself, and for the next week he was unable to think of anything except the white elephant. He went back to the Buddha and explained the predicament, at which the Buddha simply smiled. Indeed, you can spend the entire day looking for something you think you've lost, only to find that when you take off your pants to go to bed it was in your pocket all along.

Some of the most creative ideas and brilliant moments come when we are least expecting them. We must relax, let go, and not try so hard. We tend to discover the answer to a difficult relationship issue while out walking the dog, driving aimlessly on a Sunday afternoon, reading through the funnies on a lunch break, playing the 3 millionth game of Solitaire on the computer—not when we are frantically trying to come up with it in the next few minutes. It's hard to appear attractive when we're so desperate that we're frothing at the mouth.

What, You Can't Read My Mind?

When you're in a comfortable and loving relationship, you feel free to experience togetherness when you want it and free to get some distance when you need it. If it's a solid relationship, there's no harm done or offense taken, as this is the natural balancing act of daily change.

Unless you're good at it, ESP rarely works. When there's no communication between two partners, the karma starts to fly. Confusion begins to grow from the weight of so much doubt and mistrust in the air. The lack of understanding plants the seeds of frustration, and thus of suffering. As these feelings arise, we can become anxious, feel vulnerable, and then, if we're not careful, start acting defensively. Once we are acting defensively "truth" is no longer the issue, for two egos feel they've been backed into a corner.

> **KARMIC DO**
>
> Taking lots of pictures at your friend's birthday party and making him an album.
>
> **KARMIC DON'T**
>
> Taking some truly embarrassing pictures at the company holiday party and showing them around the office.

Now it is a fight over whose ego will come out on top. In order to come out on top, someone must end up on the bottom. There is no sense, just pride and vanity. Silently, we may think, "Well, I *was* kinda wrong, but now I can't admit it because I'll feel foolish." You've reached an impasse.

In a situation such as this, the karma being created by racing negative thoughts alternating between anger, revenge, guilt, and a small wish for peace does not make for an easy resolution. The cycle must be broken, and we must accept the karma we've created. Waiting for the other person to take responsibility for the whole thing so that you can divest yourself of the responsibility for your own karma only perpetuates the conflict.

We've Been down This Road Before

Couples who have been together for a long period of time often develop squabble-karma, for which they have routine scripts. They can carry them out almost on autopilot. If the relationship is shaky, these can be destructive. Once each person realizes the cues, it can become easier just to travel in the already easy-to-follow wheel ruts than to muster the energy to bushwhack a new course. But in a solid relationship, the scripts can be played out with humor and affection. The couple has learned to accept their differences, and they are no longer interested in trying to eradicate them—instead, they become a source of playful communication.

A married couple I know go through the same routine each night: She goes to bed first, and he stays up, watching TV, and inevitably falls asleep, knocking his head against

the wall behind the couch with a loud thump. She hears
it, and hollers that he should come to bed. His head comes
up with a start, and without even having to think, he loudly retorts, "I'm watching TV." Almost laughing, she yells for
him to turn it down then. He comes back with, "Shut
your door." Sometimes there's silence for another ten minutes and then the whole routine repeats itself. By 2:00
A.M., after a good snooze and with infomercials flashing in
front of his face, he lumbers down to bed. This one-act
play, once a reflection of genuine irritation between the
actors, has become a fun exchange between the two.
They've ceased trying to change one another and simply
accept their differences in lifestyle. They've turned their
one-time squabble into good karma.

Don't Crowd Me

Because within a couple relationship interdependence
takes on a concrete meaning for many, it challenges many
people's previously held belief that they were independent before the relationship. When the other person begins
to draw them into their lives, it is inevitable that those
previously held beliefs of independence become challenged on a daily basis. Suddenly there are issues of "Can't
I do anything on my own any more?" "Do you have to
brush your teeth while I'm sitting on the toilet?" "Hey,

that's my closet, you can put your stuff over in that one."
"Uh…actually, that's my side of the bed." In wanting to
be close, we also attempt not to become lost in the other

person and to retain our own sense
of self. Often, the result of this is that
as opposed to remaining "ourselves,"
we can begin to become a personal-
ity created in opposition to the
other person. Through this desire,
we can start generating bad karma.

If we maintain a sense of the
unity of everything, the situation is
easily simplified to the idea that the
way you treat others is the way in which you are treating
yourself, and vice versa.

KARMIC
DO
....
**Giving a genuine
compliment to someone
every day.**

KARMIC
DON'T
....
**Spreading gossip for the
sake of conversation.**

Am I Stuck in a Relationship Because of Karma?

Is karma keeping you with him? Or her? Or in a more
desperate relationship situation, "It?" The answer is both
"yes" and "no." Certainly a relationship is begun through
karma, and karma will either keep it going or bring it to
an end. It is up to us, not our horoscopes (unless we follow them as divine law), the other person, the sentiments
of friends, or the way we wish things would be. Things are
the way they are.

We often stay in a relationship more for the sake of the past than for any real appreciation of what's going on in the present. If we become too attached to our desire to be with someone as opposed to being alone, the feeling of being alone can become so terrifying that we'll stay with almost *anybody* simply to have a companion. No doubt, sometimes it's better to end a relationship and get a pet than maintain one to avoid aloneness.

Couples who divorce generally tend to have married under one of two conditions. They have married in haste and in a sea of emotion and fantasy, or have waited an incredibly long time before getting married because of ambiguity about their feelings for one another. In the latter case, each person was unsure and so finally they just did it to end the confusion, thinking they could work all their differences out once they had just settled down and made the decision. Ambiguous or emotionally charged karma often leads to mixed results.

> **KARMIC**
> ## DO
> ....
> Keeping a secret a friend has entrusted with you.
>
> **KARMIC**
> ## DON'T
> ....
> Telling a few others what she said because it's just so funny you can't keep it to yourself.

I'll Make It Work If It's the Last Thing I Do

Out of stubbornness or the attempt to prove something, we will often try to beat a relationship into shape, like forcing together the pieces of a poorly made assembly required desk that ends up only half-stable and needs a roll of duct tape to stay together.

We all have friends who've been telling us for weeks, months, or even years that their relationship isn't working, yet they are shocked every time we suggest that maybe they should move on. Eventually, we stop listening and consent to long conversations over lunch as long as they're paying for it.

So yes, you are in the relationship you're in because of karma, but it is not karma that is keeping you in the relationship—the only thing that is doing that is you. But the beauty of karma is that it can always be changed. Each morning when you wake up you are at the beginning of another day filled with opportunities for change. Whether it's to finally tell someone that your conversations are more like an opportunity for them to practice their monologues or to simply tell someone you've been dating that things are miserable and just not working out, you are at the helm of your own ship.

Karmic Couples

> *Love is an ideal thing, marriage a real thing;*
> *a confusion of the real with the ideal never*
> *goes unpunished.*

> —Goethe

WHILE ANY COUPLE can be described as a "karmic couple," for we are all where we are because of karma, some truly take the cake. It is the trials and tribulations of the Romeos and Juliets of the world, the Marc Antonys and Cleopatras, the Katherine Hepburns and Spencer Tracys, and more recently the Tom Cruises and Nicole Kidmans that keep us glued to the love lives of these icons of popular culture and add to the much-sought-after fairytale qualities of love. For when it comes to karma, few things are as powerful as love.

Tabloid Karma

It's been said that gossip is the glue that keeps society consistent and interdependent…well, at least for those of us glued to popular culture who sat transfixed in front of the T.V. as a white Bronco led police on a low-speed chase, and then played hookie for a week to watch O.J. stand trial. While our own lives can seem mundane and filled with the hassles of picking up the dry cleaning, reading a good headline, like "Russell Crowe Turns Women into Lesbians" or "Tom Cruise Made Relationship Contract with Penelope Cruz to Clear His Name as Heterosexual" can make our day. Regardless, the rich and famous create karma just like the rest of us—they just have the means to do it in ways that require a whole lot of money. We're obsessed, we're addicted to the karma, and just like us, so are they. If we had paparazzi following us around, it would be a prime example of collective karma at its worst.

He Said, She Said…

Who could marry Lisa Marie Presley other than Michael Jackson? Who could lure Meg Ryan away from Dennis Quaid other than Russell Crowe? Who could, at least to some extent, pull off multiple marriages with men half her age as gracefully as Elizabeth Taylor? Who could escort a Britney Spears down the runway other than a pre-pubescent boy band plastic fantastic Justin Timberlake? Who could have swept a glorious Drew Barrymore off her feet other than the ultra pseudo-actor Tom Greene…well, perhaps that's not fair.… The world's audience almost waits with bated breath for the relationships to end, and when they do, many race to be the first to say, "I told you so."

Long and short of it, the karma flying to and fro within celebrity relationships, in which fictitious personalities and public opinion play such a role and lead to inevitable disaster, are so like sixth-grade romances we can all relate to some extent—but then we can't. And so our interest is piqued. How is it that two high-profile public figures with names like J. Lo and P. Diddy become so entangled that an article entitled "Guns and Lovers" could bring it to an untimely end? Other than, perhaps, the fact that they had adopted the names J. Lo and P. Diddy? We in the "regular" universe could have guessed those names to spell ill will from the very beginning.

Change Quicker Than the Gas Price

In the world in which couples wilt more quickly than a daisy chain, we have become used to witnessing fairy-tale unions dissolve into Greek tragedies. It begs the question: Are these celebrities a perfect example of how to bring on bad relationship karma? Well, it would certainly seem so. And for $7.99, you, too, can get the astrological mating chart of Bill and Hillary Clinton and wonder at the accuracy as you compare your own relationship. But what does it actually mean? Essentially, *nothing*. For we, too, must agree that, as Freud once expressed in exasperation, "Sometimes a cigar is just a cigar."

We are in control of our own karma. *We control it.* In retrospect, we can second-guess every decision we have ever made, and when it's front-and-center in the gossip column, it seems easy to become experts on the lives of public figures. But none of us are innocent, and there is nothing for us to be innocent about. We are all living life, generating our own karma, responsible for our own karma. There is no one to blame except for ourselves for the predicaments in which we find ourselves. When those whom we analyze are public figures, there is often a glee to be found in distancing ourselves and thinking, "Oh, what a mess they just made." Thankfully, most of us don't have anybody examining our acts as closely—other than ourselves.

Love in Time

No doubt, with love only time will tell. Over the centuries, love stories have gone from ordinary day-to-day activities into the stuff of legends. And we all want the stuff of legends....

Shah Jahan and Mumtaz Mahal

In India during the early seventeenth century, the son of the emperor, Shah Jahan, a man of grandiose ambition, fell madly in love with a married woman and had her husband killed in order to wed her himself. Having ruthlessly dispatched his royal rivals, he proclaimed himself "King of the World" when he assumed the throne. To maintain his power, Shah Jahan was engaged in constant combat and military conflict. His wife, Mumtaz Mahal, whom he called the "jewel of the palace," was equally ambitious, often accompanying him on his exploits. Their karma, needless to say, was pretty intense.

KARMIC
DO
Telling the salesman you broke the vase and offering to pay for it.

KARMIC
DON'T
Quietly kicking the pieces out of the way with your foot and moving on, hoping no one saw you.

While encamped with him and his army regiment, Mumtaz died giving birth to their fourteenth child. Shah Jahan fell into a dark depression for two years, and then decided to build a fabulous monument to Mumtaz. His plan was as grandiose as he himself. The Taj Mahal took 20,000 workers, 1,000 elephants, and 20 years to build and was studded inside and out with precious jewels. Legend has it that the emperor had the chief architect beheaded and the fingers of the master craftsman chopped off so that a similar building could never be built.

Later, some say due to his extravagance, Shah Jahan was deposed by his son, who imprisoned his father in the

Red Fort—a fortress just down the river from the Taj Mahal. Shah Jahan spent the remaining days of his life there, staring at the reflection of the enormous monument to his beloved through a small mirror—and died with it in his hand. His son later entombed him alongside Mumtaz in the giant white-domed tomb. Indeed, no one escapes his karma.

Shakespeare's Star-Crossed Lovers

When it comes to love, few have chronicled as well as William Shakespeare the consequences of tragedy of those who have, in Othello's words, "lov'd not wisely but too well."

Othello and Desdemona: Othello becomes so blinded by his desire, fear, anger, and jealous love that he creates bad karma on a grand scale. It comes back at him and costs him everything he cherished. True enough, in anger we often hurt the ones we love, and thus hurt ourselves in the process. Passionately in love with his wife, Desdemona, Othello is consumed with her. His advisor, Iago, a character many consider to represent the epitome of evil, pretends to love Othello but is secretly planning to destroy him. As his tool, he uses Othello's love for Desdemona. He convinces Othello that Desdemona is unfaithful to him and in love with another man, Cassio.

Iago manipulates his wife, Desdemona's maid, Emilia, into stealing Desdemona's handkerchief, which was a gift from Othello. Iago then hides the handkerchief in Cassio's room, and the stage is set for disaster. Cassio's mistress finds the cloth and, in a jealous fit of rage, throws the handkerchief at Cassio in the presence of Othello.

Convinced of Desdemona's guilt and driven mad, Othello kills her by smothering her with a pillow from their marital bed. Emilia walks in on him, and Othello attempts to justify his atrocious act by showing her the handkerchief. Realizing what has happened, Emilia tells him the truth, and only then does Othello realize that he has just murdered his innocent and beloved wife. In despair, he stabs himself. Overwhelmed by his possessiveness and bad karma, he was unable to see things as they really were—bringing even more bad karma to bear. Although Iago had certainly played a vicious role, the end result was still the responsibility of Othello.

Romeo and Juliet: In one of the more famous love stories of all time, Romeo and Juliet are born to two feuding families: the Montegues and the Capulets. In a story of

KARMIC
DO
....
Introducing yourself and chatting with someone who is alone or seems shy at a party.

KARMIC
DON'T
....
Ignoring the person in the corner and just hanging with your friends.

true love ruled by politics, their forbidden love ends in the deaths of both lovers, who had each braved their families' mutual hatred of one another to marry. Romeo, having killed a Capulet, is banished. To stay together, a priest agrees to arrange a meeting between Romeo and Juliet at the church late one night. The priest arranges for a potion for Juliet that will give her the appearance of being dead, at which point her family brings her to the church.

Romeo, unaware of the plan, arrives at the church and finds Juliet—to his eyes, dead. In despair, he kills himself. When Juliet awakens and sees her lover dead nearby, she, too, kills herself.

Over the deaths of their children, the two families come together in mourning as they view the tragic results of the two young lovers. Watching them, the Prince of Verona says to the two families: "See, what a scourge is laid upon your hate / That heaven finds means to kill your joys with love / And I for winking at your discords too have lost / A brace of kinsmen: all are punish'd."

Edward VIII and Wallis Simpson: While these Shakespearean tragedies demonstrate the karmic results of twisted love, placing self-delusion, and arbitrary politics above love, the real-life story of Edward VIII (son of King George V) and Wallis Simpson is the epitome of choosing natural love over the trappings of power and greed. Their relationship has been hailed as one of the most dramatic love stories in modern times. To maintain the story's fairy-tale quality, we won't mention Edward's slew of mistresses prior to Wallis or the rumors that she was just after his money.

Upon his father's death in 1936, Edward was crowned the King of England, and then the troubles began. Edward was in love with a twice-divorced American woman, Wallis Simpson—a commoner. The Church of England, of which Edward was the head, could not abide his wish to marry Wallis, and the Parliament refused to give her a title. Rather than create a constitutional crisis, Edward gave up the throne—the first English monarch to voluntarily do so. Edward VIII had been King of England for only 11 months when he decided, in the name of love, to abdicate what Winston Churchill called the "greatest throne in world history."

Edward than became the Duke of Windsor, rather than King, a title that immediately went to his brother. Upon his abdication, Edward made a radio address to the nation, explaining that it would have been impossible to be King without the help and support of the woman he loved.

KARMIC DO
....
Giving a sandwich to someone who looks hungry.

KARMIC DON'T
....
Holding on to it for the rest of the day only to throw it out when you can't figure out what to do with it.

Although Wallis apparently tried to dissuade him from the move, he was determined to live his life with her. They married in 1937 and lived the rest of their lives in exile. Upon his death, Wallis commented, "He might have been a great King; the people loved him."

And Then It Just "Clicked"

CECILE CAME FROM A LONG SERIES of failed relationships and, as time progressed, she became more and more sure that the whole "true love" thing was just a fabrication created by low-end film producers in order to keep teenage romance B-flicks a viable genre. She'd done her tour of duty in relationships in which she spent too much time waiting in vain for the doorbell or telephone to ring, where silence between herself and her man of the moment was the rule while eating out because the only other option was to break up in public, and in which the words "I love you" had become about as cheap as the boxed Burgundy they were said over. While the Buddha wasn't kidding when he said that life was suffering, it seemed he may have spent one too may hours gazing at a lotus flower when he exclaimed that it could be overcome.

And then one day it happened: She fell in love. All it took was a phone call from her friend saying, "Cecile, would you mind giving my brother a ride to the airport?" and it clicked. After she had nearly given up on the idea, she met a man whose energy seemed to fill up every inside curve and niche within her. He wasn't the most attractive man she'd dated, but for some inexplicable reason every love song she used to scoff at on the radio suddenly went straight to her heart. She found herself moving through her day with a lighter step. She didn't roll her eyes any more when her friends prattled about true love over a lunch of Caesar salads.

She found herself looking forward to seeing him rather than dreading the encounter as she always had in past relationships. Everything she looked at seemed to look just a little different—the sky, clouds, streetlights, her own house. And the most unbelievable part was that just a few weeks ago *everything* had been different, and in a moment, *everything* had changed.

Moral of the story: True love exists. It's almost always under your nose or just around the corner, but the more you search for it with a magnifying glass the harder it is to see that it's "just a little up—and to the left." Karmic intent can go a long way.

RESOURCES

Blavatsky, H.P. *The Key to Theosophy.* Covina, California: Theosophical University Press, 1939.

Capra, Fritjof. *The Tao of Physics.* Boston: Shambhala, 1991.

Fields, Rick. *How the Swans Came to the Lake.* Boulder, Colorado: Shambhala, 1981.

Hart, William. *The Art of Living: Vipasana Meditation as Taught by S. N. Goenka.* Maharashtra, India: Vipassana Research Institute, 1991.

Hanson, V., R. Stewart, and S. Nicholson, eds. *Karma, Rhythmic Return to Harmony.* Wheaton, Illinois: The Theosophical Publishing House, 1990.

Klostermaier, Klaus K. *Hinduism: A Short History.* Oxford: Oneworld Publications, 2000.

Lama Surya Das. *Awakening the Buddha Within.* New York: Broadway Books, 1997.

Leifer, Ron. *The Happiness Project.* Ithaca, New York: Snow Lion Publications, 1997.

Mehta, Gita. *Karma Cola: Marketing the Mystic East.* New York: Simon and Schuster, 1979.

Rahula, Walpola. *What the Buddha Taught.* New York: Glove Press, 1974.

Rincpoche, Sogyal. *The Tibetan Book of Living and Dying.* San Francisco: Harper Collins, 1993.

Slife, Brent, and Jane Lanyon. "Accounting for the Power of the Here-and-Now: A Theoretical Revolution." *International Journal of Group Psychotherapy,* 41(2), 1991.

Watts, Alan. *Still the Mind.* Novato, California: New World Library, 2000.

ABOUT THE AUTHOR

AFTER SPENDING TIME living in India and Nepal, Joshua Mack came home to Ithaca, New York, and, inexplicably, moved from painting houses to working as a writer and editor at an Internet company in San Francisco. He currently lives in Northampton, Massachusetts, and splits his time between freelance writing and roaming the dog trails with his much-loved canine companion, Max.